THE TRUST SOLUTION

"A resourceful and clear manual for restoring trust, which should be useful for couples and for couples therapists who would like a clear process from trauma to reconnection."

HARVILLE HENDRIX, PhD
AND HELEN LaKELLY HUNT, PhD
Authors of *Getting the Love You Want: A Guide for Couples*

"With poignant case studies, Merry Frons offers much wisdom in this book on couple rupture and repair. She offers tools that help couples go beyond repair to reimagine their relationship. A helpful guide for clients and therapists alike."

SUZANNE IASENZA, PhD
Author of *Transforming Sexual Narratives:
A Relational Approach to Sex Therapy*

"*The Trust Solution* offers a detailed, step-by-step guide for couples healing from intimate betrayal. Dr. Frons' decades of experience as a couples therapist, sex therapist, and certified addictions therapist shines through each page as she eloquently gives couples key tips and tools for healing their relationship. I highly recommend this book to couples struggling with any sort of intimate betrayal."

CANDICE CHRISTIANSEN
M.ED., LCMHC, CSAT-S, CMAT-S
Founder and Clinical Director of
Namaste Center for Healing

"Thank you for giving couples a map for rebuilding trust after a marital trauma. This book is concise and focuses on the many steps to rebuild trust. I would hand it out to five couples right now!"

THERESA CALLARD-MOORE
LMSW, CST, CSAT, CMAT, MT, RMT
Founder and Clinical Director of Shanti Counseling

"Few resources address the pain of partner betrayal. *The Trust Solution* identifies the necessary steps to find strength in your relationship again. This is a must-read for anyone who has experienced infidelity!"

CAROL JUERGENSEN SHEETS
LCSW, CSAT
Author of *Help Her Heal: An Empathy Workbook
for Sex Addicts to Help Their Partners Heal*
and *Unleashing Your Power: Moving Through
the Trauma of Partner Betrayal*

"This is an excellent book for couples facing the challenge of repairing betrayal in their relationships. Merry Frons lays out in detail the steps needed to forge a new path in a fractured relationship. She does this with compassion, honesty, and realistic expectations. I highly recommend this book both for professionals working with couples and couples seeking a way back to each other."

DENISE TRAINER, MA
LCSW, NCPsyA, Psychotherapist

"In *The Trust Solution*, Merry Frons has created a road map for couples who need a solid recovery plan when one of them has violated trust and the relationship is thrown into crisis. All individuals dealing with the aftermath of this painful situation will find practical solutions, support, and wisdom in this invaluable book."

BRUCE CARRUTH, PhD
Author of *Psychological Trauma & Addiction Treatment*
and *Addiction in Human Development:
Perspectives on Addiction and Recovery*

"Kudos to Merry Frons, who's created a pragmatic, six-step guide that provides a road map for healing shattered relationships. *The Trust Solution* should be on every recovering couples reading list."

ALEXANDRA KATEHAKIS, PhD
Author of *Mirror of Intimacy:
Daily Reflections on Emotional and Erotic Intelligence*

"My marriage was over, with no hope in sight. Dr. Frons' approach was powerful. Boundaries and agreements were put into place in a gentle and effective manner. Her goal is to put you on the right path and teach you the tools to maintain a healthy relationship on your own. She taught us to hear the emotions behind the sometimes hurtful words that are blurted out in anger. And the ultimate goal is to pause before reacting when angry. She instilled this in a most effective way. Her therapy was magical in my opinion. She saved my marriage while we were in the process of a painful divorce caused by misunderstandings and poor communication. The love was still there, and she saved the marriage."

E.S., former client

"Dr. Frons has created a long-overdue, soup-to-nuts guidebook for couples impacted by infidelity and adultery. In sensitive and comprehensive prose she walks betrayed partners through their losses, grief, anger, and need for safety. Cheaters are guided toward living with the kind of integrity, accountability, and honesty required to restore relationship trust. Dr. Frons offers such couples a path toward renewed vulnerability and intimacy. I highly recommend this book for all couples who seek to move beyond—and ultimately to heal—intimate betrayal."

ROBERT WEISS, PHD
CCO / Seeking Integrity Treatment Programs
Author of Sex Addiction 101,
Out of the Doghouse, and Prodependence

——THE——
TRUST
SOLUTION

A Couples Guide to
Healing Intimate Betrayal

—THE—
TRUST
SOLUTION

A Couples Guide to
Healing Intimate Betrayal

By

MERRY FRONS, PhD

BLUE WAVE MEDIA
2021

Blue Wave Media
www.bluewave-media.com

Editorial Consultant: Joan Tapper
Book Design: John Balkwill, Lumino Press
Cover Design: Sam Frons

ISBN 978-1-7365298-0-5 (paper)
ISBN 978-1-7365298-1-2 (e-book)

First Edition
Printed in the United States of America

The case studies included in this book are a compilation of different individuals and couples. The pronouns used are simply for convenience. These issues are still based on our common humanity and transcend any divisions of sexual orientation, race, or gender.

For Marc, Alex, and Sam

"Love cannot live where there is no trust."
EDITH HAMILTON

CONTENTS

PART THREE
RENEWAL

APPENDIX

INTRODUCTION

I F YOU'RE READING this book, chances are something terrible has happened to you. Someone you love and who you thought loved you, has violated your trust by being deceitful about emotional or sexual behaviors outside of your relationship. How do you heal from the pain and loss of trust? How does a couple start to work together to repair the damage?

Couples lost in the storm of broken promises and shattered trust all too often try to heal their fractured relationship without a map. Overwhelmed by feelings of uncertainty, anger, guilt, and shame, they can't begin to find a way to repair the damage on their own. They need guidance. This book will help you through this devastating crisis in your relationship.

When the thoughts and feelings that accompany betrayal are in full force, it's difficult to imagine that there can be any chance for a transformation into something better. Some couples may even wonder if the relationship is worth saving. But there is hope—as long as both partners are willing to try. The willingness to do the work necessary for the relationship to heal is one of the first requirements. The work must also begin with the partner who betrayed the trust. Why? Because the injured party needs to be convinced that their partner has made a solid commitment to change.

My purpose is not to explain *why* betrayals happen; that's better suited for individual therapy. Betrayal can start with a seemingly unimportant action that leads down a path of lies and deception. The path is unique to every person and their experiences. What's most important—at least so far as the chances for repairing the relationship are concerned—is the attitude of the acting-out partner after their betrayal is out in the open. Do they feel terrible about what they did, or are they more upset that they were caught? (In this book, I refer to the person betrayed as the hurt partner and the one whose actions betrayed the implicit or explicit agreements of their emotional and sexual connection as the healing partner or the acting-out partner.)

Betrayal comes in many shapes and sizes. For example, information revealed without your permission or secrets kept about money, illness, and other life circumstances are common forms of betrayal. There are many more examples than we can name here, but this book focuses on the betrayal that happens when secretive actions taken by one partner—involving sexual, intimate, or romantic connections—destroy trust. This could be anything from a single instance of infidelity in an otherwise long, monogamous relationship to a hidden pornography obsession or a long series of multiple sexual encounters.

Also there can be many different kinds of relationship arrangements, implicit and explicit, between a couple. Some couples can have agreements around consensual nonmonogamy with certain rules and understandings. When those involve deceit, trust can be broken and the relationship harmed. The repair steps on Part Two can work for all kinds of relationship arrangements in many different life situations. But the focus of this book is on the agreements made in a couple relationship characterized by an understanding that they would be monogamous.

In the course of working with individuals and couples over the past three decades, I have seen many couples struggling to heal a ruptured relationship. Sometimes there was a known infidelity. Sometimes there was conflict and instability from suspicions about a lack of honesty. As I worked with clients to address these issues, I learned more about addictions, sexuality, the effects of trauma, and the dynamics of couples' relationships. I became more interested in how a relationship rupture can be repaired, and I pondered the most effective way to help individuals and couples regain trust. I found that the need for a couple to develop trust in themselves and their perceptions was just as important as regaining trust in their partners. While the circumstances of betrayal are unique for every couple, the process of healing and recovery is universal.

Unfortunately, I found very few books that I could recommend to these couples to guide them on how to work together to heal the rupture. There were books for a partner who has experienced betrayal or infidelity and books for betrayers who were struggling with addictive issues that included infidelity. Yet repairing a relationship demands that both partners commit to the process, and that requires a clear understanding of what specifically is involved. Outlining that process in a clear, accessible way is what I have tried to do in these pages. I believe it fills a gap in much-needed resources for couples who want to repair a relationship in crisis. This book does not make automatic assumptions about who is the betrayer and who has been betrayed. It is also meant for couples of all sexual orientations.

This book is not a replacement for individual, group, or couples therapy. It is a resource couples can use together while working with their therapists. However, just because both attend therapy sessions doesn't mean that both are truly willing to do what it takes to restore trust. I've seen many couples go through the motions but fail to take the necessary actions to fully heal. Sometimes one partner may merely want to restore peace and calm and alleviate their partner's distress. The commitment to stay the course and learn about themselves, their fears and vulnerabilities, and their strengths, is what makes all the difference. As both parties work through these challenges, they will become aware of the below-the-radar dynamics in their relationship, and they will understand how to rebuild the foundation of their connection.

Repairing trust, healing hurt, and establishing transparency and accountability are broad concepts. Putting them into action every day is difficult, and it is exactly where so many people need help. The steps outlined in this book fill the need for specific information to supplement and enhance the therapy process.

For this process to work, both partners need to be honest with themselves. Out of that honesty will come a shared foundation for mutual trust where words and actions are grounded in a clear understanding of what both partners value most.

There will be changes and modifications that happen for both individuals over time. I emphasize that the hurt partner does not need to make any permanent decisions about the relationship right away. I also want to underscore that each situation is different in its own way, and there is no right or wrong absolute choice. Some hurt partners may decide to end the relationship or have very clear and firm boundaries for permanent limited engagement. Others will chose to go through a healing and transformative process with their mate that can result in a better relationship than they have ever experienced. The steps in this repair process will yield valuable information for both partners to inform their choices for the future.

The Trust Solution is designed to be used by both partners. Couples can use this book together to understand the stages of an effective repair process. Or each partner may refer to it separately.

Part I is aimed at the hurt partner, the partner who has been betrayed. It explores the emotional uncertainty of that partner's situation and details how to begin to understand what happened and what steps are needed to cope and get support. This section also examines the considerations for continuing the relationship: The hurt partner needs to gain some stability. The healing partner who has caused the hurt needs to understand the impact of their actions and why the steps in Part II are necessary.

Part II is for the couple, with the focus on *how* the healing partner must take the lead in initiating repair. Here we cover the six steps that the couple will go through to regain trust and create a new, more resilient relationship. The Trust Solution is a process—a series of skills and tools—that each partner will learn to help determine if the relationship can be saved, and if so, how to repair and revitalize it.

Of course, life is not always as tidy as a how-to manual. The steps are not like grades in school. Think of them as stages that a relationship must go through, with nuances and gray areas rather than clear-cut demarcations.

Part III is about enhancing mutuality and intimacy for the future.

Throughout the book there are stories of couples who have faced the challenges of a rupture—from betrayal through a renewed relationship. They are there to illustrate aspects of the process of repair. There are also tools, exercises, self-reflections, and action items. The Appendix recaps the tools, and after that there are sections of recommended reading and a list of other helpful resources.

I admire the commitment and courage of individuals willing to confront their mistakes. I have dedicated my practice to learning the most effective tools for creating an honest and intimate connection and to helping others communicate with openness, understanding, and empathy. This book is the result of that work. My hope is that it will offer a clear process not only for a couple attempting to repair their relationship after intimate betrayal but also for therapists who work with such couples.

The journey can be difficult, as building strength often is, but the rewards are enormous. Many people have made the arduous journey back from betrayal, emerging stronger and wiser from one of life's most painful and difficult challenges. It is my profound hope and belief that readers of this book will be among those who have the ability to heal together if they choose.

To preserve confidentiality, I have made the case studies included here a compilation of different individuals and couples. The pronouns used are simply for convenience. These issues are still based on our common humanity and transcend any divisions of sexual orientation, race, or gender.

PART ONE
RUPTURE

"Not everything that is faced can be changed,
but nothing can be changed until it is faced."
JAMES BALDWIN

"You gain strength, courage and confidence by every experience where you look fear in the face."
ELEANOR ROOSEVELT

CHAPTER ONE

FACING THE CRISIS

THE UNTHINKABLE has happened: Someone you love has betrayed you by having a romantic or sexual relationship with someone else. Perhaps you had your suspicions, or you may have been caught entirely off guard. It makes little difference. Everything you thought you knew about your partner and your relationship has dissolved in an instant. You relied on this person for love and support. Now there are only feelings of confusion, anger, fear, sadness, uncertainty, and self-doubt.

The first step for you, the hurt partner, is to deal with the emotional upheaval of the betrayal. You need to ground yourself in the safety of a supportive environment where you can sort through the pieces of your shattered world. You need time to make sense of the emotional chaos surrounding you. If you are not sure what has actually happened and are still in a state of disbelief, you will need help examining your conflicting fears and suspicions. It is not uncommon to find yourself in the midst of a grief process for the many losses that you are experiencing before your brain can even begin to calculate the damage. You may question yourself and your judgment. You will cycle from denial and anger to sadness and bargaining before you can accept this new reality.

The pain is intense. You may burst into tears at any moment, your heart continually aches, your mind is often foggy, your energy has disappeared, and nothing seems stable or safe. Feelings of rage beyond what you have ever felt alternate with despair. You discover frightening parts of yourself, perhaps shouting hurtful words, slamming doors, and making threats, or binging on foods you would normally never allow yourself to eat as your anger swirls in what seems like a never-ending trap of grief. You are so flooded with emotions that it's difficult to make any decisions or make sense out of what you are experiencing.

The traumatic experience of discovering an intimate betrayal by the person you love leaves you in a tailspin where you know you need help. Ordinarily the first person you would turn to is your partner. Even while you suspected something was amiss, a part of you gave your partner the benefit of the doubt, wanting to believe they wouldn't lie or betray you. But they did, so now what?

Your natural inclination is to try to find out exactly what happened. Is your partner in love with someone else, or was it just a casual fling? Or perhaps you've uncovered an affair that has been going on for years or a long pattern of sexual acting out. Realize that you are unlikely to discover the whole truth at once.

You don't need to face this alone. You can find qualified therapists to help you. (I've listed a number of useful resources at the end of this book.) A therapist who specializes in relationships, sexuality, and intimate partner betrayal will have the experience necessary to help you recognize the situations in which you have control and assist you in determining the next right steps. They can provide a safe place where you can make sense out of the grief stages.

A support group for those facing relationship challenges or for partners of someone with an addiction—alcohol or sex, for example—also offers a safe place to share your worries and gain insight. With the group's help, you can make the right choices for good boundaries that you couldn't achieve on your own. Telling your story to a "fair witness"—someone who can hear it with compassion and empathy—will aid you in navigating these emotional times. And by hearing others' experiences, you'll receive validation of your feelings and perceptions and learn how others managed when they felt stuck or powerless. Finding the right group is an important part of the healing journey. Fortunately, there are many retreats and workshops available that can help people of all orientations and specific needs.

One caveat: Although you need support, it's important to make thoughtful decisions about whom you turn to. It's not a good idea to impulsively reveal your feelings and suspicions or any concrete evidence to family members or friends until you have had time to assess the potential ramifications. You can't take back information once it's been revealed.

The following story illustrates a hurt partner's discovery of a betrayal and her immediate reaction.

Mai and Ryan (Part 1)

Mai had asked Ryan to attend couples therapy because they couldn't seem to talk about the growing disconnection Mai felt in their relationship. After their children had left for college, the void became even more apparent. Ryan agreed to couples counseling, but the sessions often devolved into arguments in which they aired their grievances with each other. Their therapist thought that Ryan might be depressed and suggested he continue to attend some solo sessions. After a while, however, Ryan stopped going.

Nothing seemed to really shift in their relationship. Mai still felt frustrated, and the therapist suggested a group for women concerned about problems in their relationships. Mai found comfort and support hearing how the other women were coping with their relationship struggles. She started to pay more attention to things that she had taken for granted, such as family finances, and she began to notice significant cash withdrawals from their account, along with some strange charges on their credit cards, including some that dated back a few years.

When she questioned Ryan about these expenses, his explanations sounded strange. One night before Ryan got home from work, Mai decided to check his computer, trying different combinations of passwords until one finally worked. There she discovered texts and emails from escort services and a history of sexual acting out that went far beyond what she had ever imagined possible. She felt numb. She was in shock. Slowly other emotions flooded throughout her body—panic, pain, and disbelief. When she heard Ryan come through the front door, she felt a surge of anger-fueled adrenaline at the thought of him acting like everything was normal. As he walked into the

bedroom, all she could whisper was, "How could you?"
When Ryan saw the screen, he started to talk rapidly, but Mai refused to listen.
"Don't speak to me right now— just get out! I can't even listen to some explanation because I can't imagine anything that you could say that could make any sense to me!"

THE TRAUMA OF DISCOVERY

From the time when you first perceive a problem, and as you discover evidence of your partner's secrets, the need for more information builds. This is all part of the unconscious bargaining we encounter in the stages of grief. You hope you might find something that will provide a different explanation to ease the pain. As you try to make sense of the flood of emotions and sort through the information you already know, you will feel a desperate need to know more about the nature of the betrayal—how, when, how often, and with whom.

This drive to establish certainty and control pushes many betrayed partners to become relentless and obsessive about trying to uncover every lie. It's normal to try to push your mate to reveal all the details about things they have done. And it's understandable that when someone has lied to you, knowing the truth is very important. The healing process can't proceed without knowing what happened.

You may feel you will gain safety through knowing all of the details of the betrayal. But be forewarned: While you can demand to know all of the details when you first discover the betrayal, the unfortunate truth is that the betrayer rarely reveals all of the information immediately. You need to accept the fact that the whole truth will be revealed gradually, even though that may be more painful than learning about everything all at once. Though it is probably impossible to shut down your questions and desire for answers, it is better to manage this with a formal

---

While you can demand to know all of the details when you first discover the betrayal, the unfortunate truth is that the betrayer rarely reveals all of the information immediately.

"disclosure process," facilitated by a therapist. We will discuss the disclosure process in greater detail later in the book. That doesn't mean there is nothing you can do now. Taking action is often an effective antidote for feeling powerless.

You can make a bottom-line request that has certain immediate conditions such as the need for physical separation or certain information. But finding answers about what you have discovered will not give you the safety you seek. Boundaries are a way of creating safety and taking care of yourself. Nonnegotiable boundaries can be used for self-protection by establishing certain conditions that must be met for any continuing relationship, though to establish boundaries, you do need to understand your own needs and vulnerabilities. The period after discovery of betrayal is usually a time when you have the power to set nonnegotiable expectations of your partner about your immediate needs and what contact you are willing to have at this point. Some examples include requiring that your partner get professional help, attend a 12-step group, sleep in another room or another location for a certain period of time, and end all contact with any affair or sexual partners.

You need to carefully consider your emotional and physcial boundaries with your partner until they are ready to join you in the repair process. They must be ready to be truthful and transparent in *all* communication between the two of you and stop the behaviors that have led to the betrayal. You can't control another person's behavior. You can only tell them how it will affect you and your choices.

Moreover, getting more information about the betrayal will never be enough to satisfy what is driving your quest—the need for predictability, safety, and trust. There are only two ways to have those needs met: Either you and your partner must go through the painful, yet ultimately rewarding, process of repairing the relationship, or you must end it. If there is going to be a future relationship with your partner, they need to take responsibility for their actions. They need to be willing to do the steady work to repair the trust with a dedication to honesty that is consistent over time.

Sue Johnson, the founder of Emotionally Focused Therapy (EFT), identifies the three main attachment needs we have of a mate: Am I valued, can I count on you, and can I believe you? To repair the broken trust after intimate betrayal, you need more than just trust that a certain behavior or action won't happen again. You need to trust that your partner will demonstrate that they value you and the relationship. Rebuilding trust and healing from betrayal is a process—a discrete series of steps to be followed in a particular order to create a secure platform that meets these overarching needs and maximizes your chances of success.

"Three things cannot be long hidden: the sun,
the moon and the truth."
BUDDHA

CHAPTER TWO

LIFTING THE FOG

BETRAYAL IS REVEALED in different ways. Sometimes it's a looming, uncertain presence that lingers in dark corners of your mind, appearing and disappearing like a cloud that moves across the sun. You can't really see the true outlines of the problem or where it begins and ends. While you are busy with daily life—making dinner, driving the kids to activities, going to work, and dealing with professional challenges—you have no idea that anything is amiss until there is a sudden discovery: a text message on your partner's phone that says, "I miss you"; a series of unexplained credit card charges; or cash withdrawals from your joint checking account. Or there can be a creeping sense of uneasiness as absences grow more frequent with explanations that seem somehow off—"having drinks with clients, stuck working with the team." Your lack of confidence in yourself and your judgment vacillates with the hope that there was just a temporary disconnection or that your partner is experiencing difficulties with their job.

Like a glimpse of something moving under the surface of the water, the occasional sightings of disconnection leave you wondering if there's really something there or whether it's just your imagination. Your senses are receiving information that is incompatible with the beliefs you had about your life. Your mind won't acknowledge the new information. All you know is that something is off, but you can't figure out a reason for the sudden sense of distance or lack of sexual interest from your partner.

So what do you do when you don't know exactly what's causing this disturbing sense that something is wrong? You may find yourself making excuses for troubling behaviors because you want to trust and give your mate the benefit of the doubt. You may be grappling with denial, thinking your partner would never lie by saying it was a business trip when it wasn't. You may be rationalizing by thinking, "Her job requires that she attend the event without me," or "He wouldn't lie to me," or "She lies *sometimes*, but I know she really loves me."

Cutting our partners some slack can be a positive quality for a relationship, but if they aren't trustworthy, that attitude can obscure and delay the disclosure of the truth. If you try to discuss your concerns without accusation or blame, and your partner gets angry, that's often a sign that there's something they are trying to conceal.

If you are rationalizing and making excuses for your partner or blaming yourself, other people's perspectives can help. Your group and your therapist can help you try to connect the dots so you can face difficult realities. By detaching a bit from your emotions, you can focus on observing the data and examining it with the help of supportive and knowledgeable people.

The fog will begin to lift as your feelings are validated, and you can start viewing the situation with support.

IDENTIFYING THE PROBLEM

Couples therapy can be frustrating when there is no clear explanation—or there are many explanations—for the lack of intimacy, connection, and other troubling behaviors. The behaviors may be attributed to depression, where one loses interest in previously pleasurable activities; ongoing conflict and tension in the relationship; lingering resentments; or an unacknowledged sexual preference for a different gender.

Couples therapy does not usually identify a pattern of compulsive or problematic sexual behavior. When someone is in the grip of these compulsive behaviors, the lack of honesty runs deep, and the use of psychological defenses such as minimization, denial, and rationalization becomes habitual and automatic. The full extent and depth of this problem is often revealed only when some of the behaviors are discovered.

You may see your partner's history of viewing pornography on the computer but not be aware that it has reached a level of compulsion—the only way your partner can deal with uncomfortable emotions. Or you may see strange charges on a credit card but accept your partner's explanations for them. Spouses are often kept in the dark with sex addiction because it thrives in secrecy.

You don't have to identify your partner's behaviors as sex addiction to gain an understanding of what problematic or compulsive sexual behavior may look like. The World Health Organization has classified compulsive sexual disorder (CSBD) with a diagnostic code and defines it as a "central focus of the person's life to the point of neglecting health and personal care or other interests, activities, and responsibilities."

Compulsive sexual behavior disorder or sex addiction (I use these terms interchangeably) does not refer to enjoying different forms of sexual arousal or experiences or having preferences that are not recognized by the dominant cultural norms. There are many different values and attitudes about what is sexually enjoyable or acceptable. Looking at pornography while masturbating doesn't make someone a sex addict. Those are choices that healthy people can make.

Consulting with a therapist such as a certified sex addiction therapist (CSAT) who has expertise in these areas can be a way of examining all possibilities. These therapists have assessment tools and training to evaluate the presence of certain characteristics of compulsive sexuality. Your confusion will begin to lift as your feelings are validated, and you can start viewing the situation with support.

Denial, gaslighting, and bargaining all act as smoke screens that obscure what can be at the bottom of ongoing disconnection.

The term "gaslighting" comes from the 1944 film *Gaslight,* in which Charles Boyer played an evil husband who manipulates events to cause his wife, Ingrid Bergman, to think she is going insane. Your partner may try to make you believe that you didn't see what you thought you saw, that you are jealous, paranoid, or crazy. When someone gaslights you, you begin to doubt your own perceptions and continue to question yourself until you don't know what to believe. A partner who plants ideas that cause you to doubt your judgments is using a form of psychological manipulation and abuse.

Sometimes the door opens to a discovery that hits with the force of a tornado. Being blindsided by information on a computer screen or phone can change your reality in a minute. You struggle to come to grips with what seems impossible. You fall into a state of denial as your mind protects you from pain that is too intense to take in all at once. It is precisely at these moments when you are most susceptible to being gaslit. This internal struggle to grasp what seems impossible, made more difficult by a partner with a vested interest in hiding the truth and making you believe a lie, can go on for months or sometimes even years.

Some people have a single affair, which can have devastating consequences. But what do you do if you have stumbled across evidence that your partner might be guilty of multiple affairs and other types of sexual behavior? In other words, what if they have a compulsive sexual disorder? How do you know if the problem goes deeper than a single incident? There are several warning signs: online activities and

---

Denial, gaslighting, and bargaining all act as smoke screens that obscure what can be at the bottom of ongoing disconnection.

---

searches for sexual opportunities; searches for and discussions about sex in chat rooms; search for live sex webcams, websites, escort services, or other venues. Viewing pornography online may be considered by some to be typical behavior. It becomes a problem when it involves deception and severely impacts the couple's connection. If your partner is spending hours during the day or night viewing porn, that's a red flag. Your partner may suddenly close windows on his computer when you walk into a room. They may be irritable when they are not able to access or use the sexual outlet that they rely on for dealing with difficult emotions.

39

Whenever life throws addicts a curveball, they will feel a desperate need for their substance or behavior of choice, whether it's a drug, alcohol, gambling, disordered eating patterns, or sex. The substance or behavior becomes more important than the people they love. These addictions take over the addict's life and have more importance than any relationship. In recovery, however, an addict gains freedom from the prison of these preoccupations and cravings.

Clinicians agree that compulsive sexual behaviors are damaging to the individual and their relationships, although the names they use for these behaviors and their approaches may differ. The important thing is not to become entangled in nomenclature—whether they are called sex addiction or out-of-control sexual behaviors. As we said earlier, if what you are seeing matches certain criteria, then you need to educate yourself and get advice from experts.

If you have not discovered anything concrete but have suspicions, it's important to pay attention to your instincts and closely observe your partner. Your support group and therapist will impartially help you sort through your perceptions. They can analyze the information with you and help formulate an immediate plan for your physical and emotional safety and well-being. Also, it's important to get medical tests if you suspect that your partner might be sexually active outside your relationship. Unfortunately, this is often how the problem is discovered.

When the acting-out behaviors have been compulsive, there cannot be any joint recovery process until the betraying partner breaks through denial and takes responsibility for the turmoil their actions have caused. When they accept responsibility and connect their problems, excuses, secrets, and lies to their compulsive behaviors, they can then begin to accept the idea that they need help to stop.

Patrick Carnes, whose groundbreaking work has identified and created an effective treatment for sex addiction, says breaking through denial is the first task for recovery. If the addict is not open to the need for treatment and support tailored specifically for this issue, it's best for you to create strong boundaries for yourself and not join in trying to repair the relationship at this time. As long as your mate has the illusion that their will power is enough to change their behaviors, the prognosis for long-term results is not good. Patrick's daughter, Stefanie Carnes, one of the foremost experts in sex addiction, says that if the addict remains active, it is not advisable to remain living together.

The example of Camille and Brad illustrates the confusion that can arise from the discovery of sexual betrayal and how a support group can help.

Camille and Brad

Camille was looking forward to spending two weeks in the country with Brad, away from the oppressive heat and humidity of August in the city. They had quickly settled into a routine—trips to a nearby farmers market in the morning and a leisurely lunch by the pool in the afternoon. Several evenings during the week, Brad would attend AA meetings at a church in a small town a few miles away. He never said much about them, and Camille didn't ask, respecting his privacy, especially about something as fragile as his recovery.

One evening Camille thought she might find out when Brad would return by looking on his computer for a notice of the AA meeting he had said he was attending.

She found something else instead—search after search for escort services and emails and messages arranging meetings with women. Shocked, Camille called a cab to get to a car-rental place and hurried back to the city. She made it back in time to meet with her support group for relationship issues later that evening.

Arriving at their therapy suite, Camille paused, trying to collect herself. Inside, the other members waited, perched on chairs and sofas, iced coffees and lattes at hand. All chatter stopped as their therapist opened the door and motioned them inside the spacious, light-filled office with soothing landscape photos on the walls.

Their therapist turned to Camille, "Do you want to talk about it?"

"I'm not even sure I should have driven here," Camille said, pulling off her sunglasses to reveal red, bloodshot eyes. "I felt so shaky, but I had to get out of there. I drove back to the city this morning." Her face was pulled into a tight mask of despair.

Another member of the group touched her arm and nodded, encouraging her to open up. "Camille, what happened?" Everyone waited for a minute for her to continue.

"I guess I've had this sense for a while that something was off, and that's what made me seek out this group. I don't know if I was ignoring red flags, or I was just so caught up in growing my business that I wasn't paying enough attention to what Brad was doing. I never thought it could be something so extreme.

"It all feels surreal. Look at these." Her hands shook as she pulled a bunch of computer printouts out of her bag. There were copies of emails, credit card receipts, and hotel invoices.

"How could he do this?" Camille asked, choking back the tears. "It's like I don't know who this person is. He said he was at AA meetings, but these show that he was meeting women. This is absolutely crazy. How could I have not

42

seen any of this? The woman he claimed was an old girl-friend is actually a sex worker. He was continuing to see her along with these other women while we were supposed to be on a vacation together, and I sat waiting for him to get back frm what he said were his AA meetings."

The other women wanted to ask more, but they recognized that Camille needed to express the confusing and painful mix of emotions that were hitting her all at once. This was only the third meeting of the support group that Camille had attended, and the others didn't know much about the history of her relationship.

"We met when he hired my company for a big account with his business, but I didn't get involved with him until the contract ended. We could talk about anything, and I thought I'd finally found the one. I talked with my therapist about him. I thought it was a good sign that Brad said he had been in recovery for five years and was active in AA. I thought it showed self-awareness. We had big dreams together. I felt like he believed in me.

"The only thing that I felt concern about was that he was hesitant about marriage. He said he was discussing it with his therapist. I knew he had been married before. He told me that she left him for someone else. After six months we moved in together. Actually, if I'm being truthful, there was another concern. There was a woman that he had been involved with. He said she was an ex-girlfriend. He never introduced us, and he never mentioned seeing her, so I really didn't feel any threat from this. I think I assumed if he was getting together with her that he'd mention it."

The other women exchanged knowing looks, waiting to hear what had happened.

"We were in the country, and he started to have these absences. We had rented a house for two weeks to get out of the city. Brad said he was going to AA meetings. It *was the first time we were together for two weeks without either of us working, and I thought he was just adjusting to a different meeting schedule while we were there. This morning I noticed he had left his computer open, with a document he had been working on when he rushed out the door. So I looked to find out which town had the AA meeting I thought he had gone to, wondering what time he would get back. I can't believe what I found."*

"Was he meeting his ex?" a group member asked.

"No, it was much worse. He'd been searching for sex partners close to where we were staying. I started digging some more. He was searching for sex connections at the very times when he told me he'd been going to AA meetings. I suddenly felt that I didn't know who he was and what I was dealing with.

"I felt totally panicked that he would come home any minute. I printed out copies of the stuff I found. I copied some things to a flash drive. He had the car so I took an Uber to the car-rental place. It felt like a scene in a horror movie where the victim is trying to escape from a maniac."

The words were spilling out breathlessly. "He started to text me as soon as he got to the house and saw I wasn't there. He kept asking where I was. I didn't respond until about the 20th text. I texted him some of what I had found, but I didn't want to tell him everything. I wanted to see how truthful he would be, so I didn't want to reveal my full hand.

"At first, he tried to deny everything and made some crazy explanations. But I guess he figured out that I knew something that would cause me to take off like I did. After he saw that I wasn't buying his explanations, he finally admitted that he had seen his ex-girlfriend. But he said it was a couple months ago. He still tried to say that he was at AA meetings, talking to some guys that needed help! I couldn't believe it!

"He kept saying I needed to come back, and we could talk. He told me to calm down. What was he thinking? Does he really think I'm that stupid?

"I can't think straight. I don't know what to do. I feel really scared, like I don't know him at all. Even now I don't really understand the extent of this. I'm worried that this could be just the tip of the iceberg. We have separate finances, so I'm limited in what I can see, but from what I did find I'm sure he's been seeing escorts."

Camille sat back, exhausted. It was as if she'd experienced the discovery of Brad's deception all over again. The group responded with murmurs of condolence. They'd all experienced something like this.

The therapist placed a hand on Camille's shoulder. "I think we all want to support you in creating a major boundary here and getting yourself out of this as cleanly and quickly as you can."

Although she wasn't able to understand it at the time, Camille was on her way to her own recovery. She would soon learn that, with time, the trauma of the experience fades, leaving just the outlines of the learning she can take forward to create a better life.

In the days and months after discovery your focus needs to be on providing safety for yourself in order to manage the trauma response. There will be different requirements that depend on the circumstances. In Camille's situation, she needed to cut off all contact in order to create safety and soothing for herself. Your support system and therapist will help you determine what your needs are during this time.

The next chapter focuses on the skills that help that movement forward.

"Human beings, by changing the inner attitudes of their minds, can change the outer aspects of their lives."
WILLIAM JAMES

CHAPTER THREE

CALMING THE STORM

T HE DAILY UPS AND DOWNS will be unpredictable. That's part of what makes this time period so hard. You never know when the emotions will hit you—as you pick out breakfast cereal in the supermarket or when you settle down to relax in front of the television. There will be certain situations, perceptions, or memories that will unleash an eruption of anger or sadness seemingly out of nowhere. You will need strategies and tools to help you cope with intense emotions and feelings of helplessness that make it difficult to make a simple decision or take even a small step forward.

It's helpful to understand *why* you are often blindsided by these feelings. The unconscious mind is always scanning our environment for safety or danger, recognizing patterns to help us react quickly to situations where it perceives a threat. Sometimes a situation can trigger painful memories or emotions when what's happening in the present has something in common with a past event. It could be a taste, a smell, a quality of light, or something completely outside our awareness that reminds us of a painful memory or feeling. Gaining insight into what produce these reactions will allow you to arm yourself with tools to use when you encounter these unexpected triggers.

You will need safety with people, places, and things. Creating a safe space in your immediate environment to start the day can be done by creating a morning ritual.

You will need safety with people, places, and things. Creating a safe space in your immediate environment to start the day can be done by creating a morning ritual, for example, grabbing a few minutes for yourself as you ride to work or do other morning tasks. Perhaps the most important touchstone in your week will be knowing that there is also a place of safety for you to retreat to and gather strength, such as a therapist's office or a group meeting.

TOOLS

TOOLS FOR SOOTHING

Breathing

This is the classic tool for soothing. Notice your breath by inhaling to the count of three, hold for two seconds, then exhale to the count of four. Breathe in deeply and slowly, hold, and then breathe out. You can repeat to yourself "re" as you breathe in and "lax" when you exhale.

Do this several times a day to help center and calm yourself.

Mindfulness

Notice and identify your range of feelings and perceptions without judging them or trying to push them away. As a way of detaching from them, imagine yourself standing a bit apart from the emotions, sensations, or impulses and see them as something separate from you.

Name Feelings

Putting names to the various feelings as you observe them makes those emotions more concrete and manageable. For example, it's more helpful to name feelings of disappointment, rejection, contempt, rage, or pain to help identify what you may have referred to as just anger or sadness.

Journal/Gratitude

A journal offers another place to put disturbing feelings so that you can examine them later to gain more clarity and see patterns to the triggers, cognitive distortions, and emotional reasoning.

Many clients report that it's been helpful for them to keep a gratitude journal; in the evening before bed, or at any other good time, they write down—or just think of—three things they are grateful for.

Move a Muscle, Change a Thought

This saying from 12-step programs advocates moving around, taking a walk, and getting active when disturbing feelings and thoughts occur as a way of dealing with them.

Visualization

Picture an emotion you are feeling as a wave that ebbs and flows. Imagine that emotion subsiding like a wave, or picture yourself surfing the wave and swimming to safety as the water subsides.

Safe Place

This is another visualization tool. Close your eyes and picture a place—it can be real or imagined—that is peaceful and safe. Some clients see a beach, a lake, or a room with a fireplace and objects that feel comforting. When a disturbing emotion hits, picture yourself in this safe place.

Container

This is a third tool using visualization. Close your eyes, and visualize a container that has a lid or something that can be regulated when you want to release what's inside. For some it might be a basket with a lid, for others a metal drum with a valve, or even a Tupperware container. You could picture an iron drum with a solid seal or a wicker basket with a lid. Simply imagine an object in which you can seal in disturbing thoughts and emotions as they come up. Visualize the unpleasant material being tucked inside and held there until you choose to look at it with your support group or your therapist. When you do pull out those perceptions and thoughts, they will probably have lost a bit of their power. You and your support team can figure out how you can best utilize this information. There will be new insights and learning that will increase your healing in spite of the pain.

Awareness of Triggers

Our brains developed through evolution for survival and safety, and it has become a pattern-recognition machine. Sometimes it will detect a match from the present with a painful memory outside of our awareness. By becoming aware of what stimulates the resuing flood of emotion, you will be able to better regulate those emotions and protect yourself from distress. One way to do this in by using the Cognitive Behavioral Therapy (CBT) worksheet, on which you can list what preceded the reaction and the feelings and the thoughts that came up. *An example is included here.*

CBT WORKSHEET

EVENT	FEELING	INTENSITY	THOUGHTS

Recognize Cognitive Distortions

Many people fall into the trap of thinking "because I feel something it must be true," instead of basing their conclusions on a combination of logic and emotion. It's useful to be aware of the many ways our thinking can become distorted, such as making overgeneralizations, black-and-white thinking, ignoring positive evidence, emotional reasoning, personalizing information, and even predicting catastrophes. Recognizing when your mind falls into these traps is the first step in climbing out of them.

Affirmations and Self-Talk

Use self-talk—speaking internally to yourself—to calm a painful emotion. When our limbic system or primitive brain is in the grip of strong emotions, we are not able to think clearly. Creating self-talk in those moments will be difficult, so it's helpful to have affirmations prepared that you can use when you are flooded with emotion. Preparing some useful messages, and having them handy, will be easier than making them up on the spot. Here are some examples, but these are only suggestions. Take your time to write some that have meaning for you.

SAMPLE AFFIRMATIONS

I am grateful for my health and the health of my children.

I will gently allow fear to step aside and focus on doing the next right thing for me.

I will not let anyone else have power over how I feel. I get to choose how I feel.

My past does not define who I am today. I get to define who I am today.

I do not give up when things get difficult. I know how to persevere through setbacks.

ACTION ITEMS

ACTION ITEMS FOR CALMING AND SOOTHING

- Create a list of affirmations for yourself.

- List three triggers that you have experienced or anticipate having to deal with going forward.

- Where do you feel distress in your body—your chest, your heart, your throat—when emotions grip you? Learn to be aware of sensations in your body, so you are alert to the first signals of distress and can start using coping skills.

- List three strategies you will use when you start feeling distress in your body.

- Name the disturbing feelings with specific words such as anger, confusion, disappointment.

- Identify the story you are telling yourself that comes with this feeling.

- Become aware of cognitive distortions, such as going from a specific to a generalization, that arise when disturbing thoughts appear.

*"You drown not by falling into a river,
but by staying submerged in it."*
PAULO COELHO

CHAPTER FOUR

BRIDGE TO REPAIR

I T'S NOT ENOUGH for the healing partner to simply say they want to stay together. If your relationship is going to stand a chance of being repaired, the process cannot begin until your partner acknowledges the impact their actions have had on you, the one who has experienced the betrayal. *Remorse does not equal repair.* Relationship repair is a process and must be built on a foundation of honesty. This includes the betrayer's being honest with themselves about the impact of their behaviors.

Relationship repair is a process and must be built on a foundation of honesty.

The healing partner must demonstrate commitment with agreements, accountability, transparency, and empathy that remains consistent over time. The actions and behaviors that demonstrate this commitment are outlined and explained in the six-step process in Part Two, but the

57

hurt partner doesn't need to join their partner in the healing process until the hurt partner is ready. The hurt partner will often ask, "How will I know if they are working on their recovery?" The answer: "You will see continuous and consistent behavioral changes."

While the couple is working on rebuilding trust, the hurt partner needs to keep boundaries firm and consistent and communicate clearly about these and bottom-line behaviors as a way of creating emotional safety. Nonnegotiable boundaries and conditions will provide some protection from additional hurt and give the hurt partner time to access their mate's commitment to the relationship. *These may include:*

- Stopping all contact with an affair partner

- Requiring attendance at therapy to gain insight about their behaviors

- Attending couples therapy if the nature of the betrayal is still not clear

- Agreeing to an evaluation by a CSAT for sexual addiction if that is suspected

- Attending a 12-step group or going to an in-patient treatment program

- Limiting contacts as agreed to by the hurt partner

Another requirement is often a formal disclosure process with a set date. Disclosure is where the unfaithful partner reveals all of their acting-out behaviors. In Part Two we give details about the disclosure process, which doesn't happen spontaneously. Both partners need to prepare to ensure the process is thorough and complete.

There are times at the beginning of the repair process when one partner will refuse to agree to new boundaries or merely pay lip service to their partner's requests.

Some of those issues are evident in the following story of Hiro and Lucia.

Hiro and Lucia

Hiro felt increasing distance in his marriage to Lucia. Before they left for vacation to spend time with her parents in Mexico, he tried to talk with her. She said nothing was wrong and seemed annoyed at him, as she often did these days. If he asked why she got home late from work or an event she would blow up at him. He started to notice that she kept her phone with her in ways he hadn't observed before. He saw her taking more care with her hair and makeup and what she wore to work. One night when she was in the shower, she left her phone where he could see it. He discovered many texts she'd exchanged with her colleague Robert. Hiro thought these might be connected with her emotional distancing.

He didn't want to confront Lucia right before leaving for their vacation, however, since they were staying at her parents' house. He reasoned that maybe things would improve when she was away from work and the family was all together. But when they got to Mexico, nothing changed. Even with her parents and their son around, Lucia was moody and withdrawn.

Lucia disappeared for long periods of time and continued to be distant, as though she was in her own world.

59

When she did speak with Hiro, the conversation often turned into an argument even if they were discussing something as simple as where to go for dinner.

Hiro had started to attend a support group for people dealing with relationship conflict, and he tried to use the skills he had learned from his group, for example, naming his feelings— frustration, disappointment, hurt, and yes, anger. Though he had been looking forward to this time together for months, the vacation ended up merely deepening his insecurities.

When the couple returned home, Hiro tried again to talk with his wife.

"Lucia, something's not right," he began. "I think we should talk to somebody about this."

"Hiro, why are you making a big deal out of this? I feel smothered by you," Lucia said.

Hiro desperately wanted to find a way to fix things with his wife, but he felt powerless and at a loss as to what to do. He couldn't stand the thought of breaking up their marriage, particularly since their son was only five years old.

Hiro told Lucia he had discovered her text messages with Robert and that he had overheard her whispered conversation with him when they were in Mexico.

"We need to talk with a therapist because there's a lot of tension in our relationship," he said.

But Lucia resisted. "I'm too busy at work and with our son's schedule. It's another obligation for me."

Hiro pressed on. "Something needs to change. I'm really uncomfortable about your relationship with Robert. I need to know what's going on."

"He's my closest friend at work. I'll let you know every time I see him."

This did not satisfy Hiro's discomfort. "I understand that you work together, but you aren't open with me about when you are getting together with him outside of work."

"Well, I'll report all of our interactions to you."

Hiro found himself questioning Lucia's sincerity. He continued to feel that she didn't want to give him the transparency he needed to reestablish trust. For her part, Lucia said that she had a right to some privacy and that Hiro was jealous of Robert. When she scheduled a business trip to Chicago, Hiro asked to go with her, but Lucia told him she didn't want him there. Hiro asked if Robert were going. "I have no idea," she said.

Hiro continued to feel insecure and dismissed by his wife every time he made an effort to talk with her. He found himself relying more on the support of his group, whose other members also shared information about the struggles in their relationships. The group members talked about setting different boundaries, including making bottom-line requests. Hiro began to consider what boundaries and conditions he could set with Lucia.

The group helped Hiro understand the vagueness in Lucia's responses toward him. Her unwillingness to provide transparency was causing Hiro to distrust what she told him. He finally insisted they go to couples therapy or talk about a separation. After a few sessions in couples therapy, they reached a stalemate. Lucia couldn't give Hiro the commitment he had requested.

Hiro's group supported him during this difficult time by saying things like, "Only you can evaluate the potential for moving forward, in yourself and with your partner. We are here to support what you are feeling and tell you what we see. Only you can decide what actions you are willing to take."

Over time Hiro continued to evaluate Lucia's willingness to engage in a repair process to regain trust. He was working through the difficult feelings of being in a relationship with a partner who was not willing to give much in terms of commitment, accountability, and change.

EVALUATE WILLINGNESS

As the hurt partner, you need to be aware of how your partner's participation will make or break the potential for your relationship's future. Their *actions*, not their words, will ultimately determine the decisions you make.

It is important not to relax the boundaries you have created too soon. Knowing your non-negotiables and understanding your needs during this delicate process can help you move forward, secure in the feeling that you are taking care of yourself. In the meantime, your partner must evaluate their commitment to repairing the relationship.

If your mate wants to repair the relationship, they need to own their behavior, stop making excuses, and stop minimizing their actions. They need to understand not only how to communicate remorse and a desire to help heal the pain they have caused but also commit to the specific steps they need to take for you to be willing to move forward together. The steps that I outline for the repair process apply to *any* betrayal situation in an intimate relationship, whether it was an affair, or compulsive sexual behaviors, or serious sex addition. As we meet the couples in Part Two going through the repair process, we will see some partners that demonstrate the limits on how far they are willing to go to renew trust.

There are some situations that call for immediate severing of the relationship. When there are incidents that are life threatening or involve serious crimes or continuous exploitation then stronger actions are required. In those cases it's most important to get expert advice from experienced professionals without delay.

Also, if there is no effort toward recovery on the part of the partner who was the betrayer, and especially if they are still involved in acting-out behaviors, then it isn't wise to continue to invest in the relationship. Patrick Carnes reminds us that all addictions have "people who are not able to do what is necessary." For the hurt partner, having good support systems and expert advice is crucial for supplementing your discernment skills and protecting yourself and your family.

Only *you* can evaluate the potential—in yourself and in your partner—for moving forward. Only *you* can decide when the process stalls for you and what actions you want to take.

As the wounded partner, you always need to remember that you are not responsible for your mate's actions. Remember that you don't have to make any permanent decision right away. You may feel very differently in six months or a year. During this time you will be creating safety and stability for yourself with things that you can control. This will help you determine not only your partner's willingness but your own willingness to go down the road of repair with them.

QUESTIONS FOR ASSESSMENT

- Is your partner open to your requests for treatment?
- Do they acknowledge the impact on you and respond with empathy and compassion?
- What level of commitment do they have for repairing the trust they have broken?

- Do they want to settle the immediate crisis or do whatever it takes to create a new relationship based on honesty and restored trust?

- Have they met some of your bottom-line requests, such as cutting off all contact with an affair partner or starting treatment for sexually compulsive behaviors?

- Do they want you to take any blame for their behaviors?

- Do they engage in a power struggle in which they need you to acknowledge your part in relationship problems?

- Do you feel they are willing to do whatever it takes to repair your relationship?

KEY POINTS

KEY POINTS FOR PART ONE

- Recognize the effects of trauma and the stages of grief.

- Recognize initial needs for safety, support, and soothing.

- Gain more clarity about the betrayal.

- Learn tools for safety and soothing.

- Set appropriate boundaries for engagement or separation.

- Evaluate your partner's willingness and participation in the healing and repair process.

PART TWO
REPAIR

*"Love is nothing without action.
And sorry is nothing without change."*
UNKNOWN

"All you need is the plan, the road map, and the
courage to press on to your destination."
                                        EARL NIGHTINGALE

CHAPTER FIVE

THE 6 STEPS OF REPAIR

B ETRAYAL violates one of our most primal attachment
instincts—the need for trust in our close relationships.
Whether the betrayal was a one-time transgression or
a pattern of hurtful behaviors, you can't heal the pain and
repair a relationship with a stroke of insight or a promise, no
matter how sincere, that "it will never happen again." That's
just the start. The healing partner must empathize with their
partner's needs and demonstrate their commitment to creating a new foundation for the relationship, one built on honesty, transparency, empathy, and trust.

When a couple has experienced a crisis of intimate betrayal, they view their relationship from two different perspectives. The hurt partner feels that they were not loved or
valued enough. Otherwise, how could their partner have
done these things? After this discovery, the hurt partner
is in a state of emotional turmoil where it's impossible to
identify how or even if they can heal. They are still grieving
the loss of the relationship they thought they had and are

unsure about the future.

On the other hand, the healing partner may have their own set of rationalizations about why they acted the way they did. But they need to put those feelings aside and take the lead in the repair process if they want the relationship to survive. It will take some time for the hurt partner to start believing that the person who hurt them so badly will be capable of the understanding, loyalty, and commitment that a relationship repair requires. The hurt partner will only join the healing process and participate as trust grows, and they feel safe enough to risk connection. Their focus will be on their three primary needs: "Do you value me, can I count on you, and can I believe you?"

The healing partner's demonstration of commitment, reliability, and honesty over time will create a safe meeting point on the bridge to a mutually trusting relationship.

The early stages of discovery are often the most dangerous. That's when the relationship can be broken beyond repair if one partner or both decide to call it quits. But it's also a time when couples may try to reconcile too quickly in the false belief that the acting-out partner has changed. The hurt partner is eager for things to go back to the way they were, and even some therapists I have supervised have fallen into the trap of thinking a quick repair is possible. But so much more than a behavior change is needed to heal a betrayal.

Many couples struggle to understand how the trust in the relationship could ever be repaired. Facing this crisis may seem overwhelming and even hopeless at times for both partners. Caught in the trauma of betrayal, they find it difficult, if not impossible, to gain the perspective necessary to have a vision of the future.

The steps in this repair process provide a framework for emotional growth to overcome character and emotional deficiencies that block intimacy and connection. This work needs to happen in the safe confines of a well-defined commitment with clear boundaries and expectations and a system for providing accountability and transparency.

As each partner continues with their own individual work for healing, the couple can begin to work together for a new connection based on honesty and open communication. Resetting the emotional balance in the relationship will be part of the healing and restoring of trust. This requires a platform of mutuality, which was lost when one partner made choices that caused harm to their mate and their relationship. We will talk about the needs for mutuality in Part Three. When this quality is present, decisions are made from the perspective of a two-person system, not on a unilateral basis.

The couple can learn the skills of co-regulation for emotional distress by truly supporting each other. This will require each partner to acquire good skills for emotional regulation, distress tolerance, and boundary setting, as well as skills for attunement and mutuality. These skills develop over time with a serious dedication to acquiring these skills, faith, and patience. By implementing the following steps, you can start to change your relationship.

THE SIX STEPS

1
Become Accountable

2
Be Honest

3
Create Agreements

4
Evaluate Progress

5
Improve Attunement and Empathy

6
Learn Communication and Conflict-Repair Skills

THE SIX STEPS are the bedrock of relationship repair and renewal, and we will go over each of them in detail in the chapters that follow. They provide a structure of mutually agreed-upon tasks, skills, and agreements that act as a bridge between the couple's divergent perspectives. Each step contains valuable tools that you and your partner will learn in order to restore trust, empathy, and love into your relationship.

"...there will be no healing without accountability."
THE REV. DR. EMMA JORDAN-SIMPSON

CHAPTER SIX

—STEP 1—
BECOME ACCOUNTABLE

ACCOUNTABILITY MEANS the healing partner must acknowledge how their actions hurt their partner and express remorse for the deception and betrayal. They need to hold themselves accountable for their actions and their impact, otherwise there can be no forward movement. Part of accountability is expressing regret, remorse, and apologizing for the effects of those actions. Accountability can include a statement of the intention to make restitution to the person they have hurt. But the heart of accountability is an acknowledgment of how their actions have harmed and altered the covenant of the relationship.

The healing partner needs to understand that their mate may not meet them in the repair process for quite some time until consistency, accountability, and some level of trust are established. Until that time the healing partner has to become a source of comfort, safety, and reassurance. Those behaviors will start to create a bridge for each partner to join in the healing and repair process.

Here's what accountability is not: Accountability is *not* asking for forgiveness or for the hurt partner to continue the relationship. It is *not* asking the hurt partner for anything. The healing partner acknowledges that they alone are responsible for the betrayal, that their partner didn't cause it. Accountability is not a one-time statement or apology. It's a series of ongoing actions that need to become habits embedded in the relationship:

- The healing partner needs to respect their mate's bottom-line conditions for there to be an effective repair.

- The healing partner needs to access and own their commitment to doing whatever it takes to see this process through.

- The hurt partner needs to evaluate the commitment their partner is making and consider if they are willing to work on repairing the relationship.

One can't be accountable without first being honest with oneself and others. Though the healing partner may be struggling with feelings of shame, remorse, or internal conflicts, they need to be clear about their intentions if they want to remain in your relationship. They must demonstrate the grit to stick with the relationship-repair process despite setbacks and discouragement, which are inevitable. This determination will give their mate the safety and security needed to risk moving forward.

Just as the hurt partner needs time to adjust to the new reality of the relationship, the healing partner will need to deepen their understanding of themselves, their motivations, and their true intentions. It's not just an intellectual understanding. It's an emotional learning experience where one grows in self-awareness and increases the capacity for empathy, mutuality, and honesty that a genuinely intimate relationship requires.

Having a willingness to live a life of accountability and honesty is the basis of trust. It starts with learning to tell the truth. Many 12-step programs begin with an admission: "My name is Bob, and I'm an alcoholic." This is a model of accountability. It illustrates how to own difficult parts of yourself and being able to acknowledge and accept who you are.

One tool to start this process is an accountability statement. It's a way for the healing partner to communicate their intentions and take responsibility for their actions. It helps to write it down. *Here is an example.*

"I want to express how sorry I am for the pain and damage I've caused to you and our family. I know these words can't convey the degree of remorse and regret I feel, but I want to acknowledge that my intention is to make the healing and repair of our relationship my priority. I am following the process in *The Trust Solution*, and I hope that at some point in the future we can work through these steps together."

When there is a written accountability statement, each partner can return to it. Otherwise, in painful situations like these, it can be hard to express and absorb information. Writing down what the healing partner wants to say can help avoid unnecessary misunderstandings. It's also good for the hurt partner to have a copy, in case they have doubts about their partner's intentions.

The following story illustrates how one couple's relationship began to unravel and the choices they each made.

Blair and Marcus (Part 1)

Blair felt that she and Marcus were under tremendous pressure from their jobs as political reporters. Her therapist suggested she attend a therapy group to deal with the stress and relationship issues. Blair told the group that over the past few months, Marcus had seemed increasingly irritable, criticizing her cooking and her messiness. It had gotten to the point she felt she couldn't do anything right anymore.

Another group member talked about how much pressure her partner had experienced at work, and how his drinking had gotten out of control, making him irritable and critical. She asked Blair about any other changes that had occurred in their lives recently. All it took was that question for Blair to make the connection: Mariah, a woman Marcus used to date, had returned to the newspaper about six months earlier, around the time Marcus's behavior started to change.

When Mariah first returned to the paper, Blair hadn't given it too much thought. Things were long over between them, and Marcus seemed indifferent to Mariah's return. In fact, he barely mentioned her since Blair first found out at an office party the previous summer that Mariah would be coming back.

Now Blair noticed that many of the bylines on Marcus's stories included Mariah's name. He hadn't mentioned that he was working with her that much. At her next group session, she said, "I'm beginning to wonder if Marcus hasn't been spending time with Mariah that doesn't include reporting. When he got home last night, I asked if he was working with her a lot and how much time they were spending together. He admitted he had spent time with Mariah when I visited my parents a month ago. He said he didn't want to tell me because, 'You'd blow it out of proportion. You've always had a competitive thing with her.'"

Just recounting the incident upset her. "I was angry that he seemed to be keeping his relationship with Mariah a secret," Blair said. "He said he didn't feel he had to report his interactions with every work colleague. It wasn't like him to be so defensive. Ever since then, we've been having fights about Mariah."

Blair was not one to snoop into Marcus's emails or his phone, but now her suspicions were growing. He had always talked about news stories he was working on, and those usually included anecdotes about the team. Curiosity got the best of her. Marcus was careless about his passwords, and she knew it wouldn't be hard to get into his computer. She wasn't surprised when she saw the number of texts and emails, but she didn't expect the content, which indicated that Marcus was much more involved with Mariah then he admitted.

Marcus and Blair came to their first couples therapy appointment in a state of crisis. Marcus denied that the relationship had been sexual and said that he was just trying to avoid conflict. "Mariah's emails indicate a different story, Marcus," Blair said. "I can't stand you lying to me. You have to figure out what's important to you. For now, you can stay with your friend Josh until you figure out what you want."

Marcus said that what he wanted was to repair their relationship. Blair recalled her group talking about their partners' needing to take responsibility. Some of the other *group members had regretted not learning the truth all at once, instead of it coming out in dribs and drabs. "I don't want you staying in the apartment. Not knowing the truth is just too painful for me to even be around you."*

Though the truth hurt, Blair thought it could have been worse: Marcus and Mariah had not slept together, though Blair believed that would have happened had she not intervened when she did. Blair told Marcus she needed some time to think things over. She saw her individual therapist regularly, and she also got support from her group. Hearing how other women had repaired their relationships after traumatic betrayals gave Blair hope.

Marcus also drew support from his group and worked at establishing better accountability and transparency with Blair. He started to understand how he had to end any involvement with Mariah and be prepared to deal with her reactions, which he knew would be painful. He saw that he had crossed a line that he had never intended to cross by making what his therapist called "seemingly unimportant decisions." The men in his group challenged Marcus when he told them that he had agreed to work with Mariah at his apartment when Blair was out of town. "What were you thinking, man?" they asked Marcus. "Mariah made it clear that she wanted to resume where you left off, and you opened the door. People won't observe boundaries unless you give them the right signals."

Accountability, in addition to taking responsibility for the harm of one's actions to others, lays a groundwork for eventual mutual healing, growth, and support that benefits both partners. The prodependence model, developed by Rob Weiss, advocates for an attitude of compassionate support and love for a partner who is struggling to repair the damage they have caused to their relationship when they have taken accountability for the harm their actions have caused.

The hurt partner, by using protective boundaries, can be clear about how and when they can engage, with the goal of mutual healing and growth for both partners. The compassion of the prodependence model is based on the understanding that we all have our areas for growth and handicaps from our wounds. As Weiss states in *Prodependence: Moving Beyond Codependency,* "We are all wounded in one way or another. No one makes it to adult life without some well-earned emotional and psychological battle scars. Some of us have more of them.."

Over time the hurt partner will observe the level of accountability and evaluate the healing partner's commitment to repairing the relationship. It does not bode well for the future of the relationship if accountability is lacking or inconsistent. In the stories of the couples we encounter in this book, we can see the negative consequences when accountability is limited. It will be clear that some partners were unwilling to do what was needed or to see the process through to restore trust. Others, however, stayed the course and repaired their relationship. The hurt partner has to understand their own feelings about maintaining a relationship with a partner who is neither wholly accountable nor honest. There is no need to make any irrevocable decisions at this point. Not every couple can make it. It takes a lot of resilience and courage to go through this journey.

In the story of Jason and Mac we see how Mac did not have the willingness, self-awareness, and understanding for being accountable in his relationship with Jason. He lacked discernment about the transparency that accountability requires as he avoided disclosure and continued to keep secrets.

Jason and Mac (Part 1)

Mac was a celebrity chef at one of Brooklyn's hottest new restaurants. He met Jason at a wine tasting and remarked that Jason had offered the best organic burgundy he had tasted that month. Flattered, Jason suggested they promote his wine at Mac's restaurant. Jason's wine distribution business was on the way to becoming successful, but Mac's connections could really push his business over the top.

Mac arranged for Jason to meet his sommelier. Soon they had a private tasting with two other popular restaurant owners, along with their sommeliers and some friends. Some of Jason's wines were added to the menus of popular restaurants owned by Mac's friends. Jason and Mac began spending most of their time together, even though it was difficult with Mac's work schedule. They would drive up to Jason's country house in the Hudson Valley early on Sunday morning and spend two days enjoying their mutual passions for gardening, cooking, and wine.

Their circle included other people from the restaurant world, and every weekend would revolve around the production of an extravagant meal. They all tried to outdo each other with their culinary skills, and Jason always provided the wines to pair with the gourmet meals. He was happy their lives were merging together and thought this might be a relationship he could settle into. Even though they hadn't talked about exclusivity, Jason just assumed they were in sync from the amount of time they spent together. But one Saturday night, when a group of their friends had gathered, they began trading stories of past and present exploits. After several bottles of wine had loosened Mac up, he shared several uncensored stories. Jason felt an uneasy sense that something wasn't right.

The next morning Mac was feeling hung over and suggested a ride to the farmers market might do them both some good. Even though the fresh air sounded nice, Jason decided to stay home, saying he had work to do.

A few minutes after Mac left, their friend Jeff knocked on the front door. He was bearing a basket full of fresh tomatoes. "We got way too many of these. Can you use them?" he asked. "They'd be great for Mac's famous gazpacho."

"Sure," Jason said. "Want some coffee? Mac just took off for the farm stand."

After putting the tomatoes on the counter, Jeff lingered, gazing out the window at the garden for a few minutes. He seemed to have something on his mind. "So, a couple weeks ago, you went to see a musical. You like it?"

"Yeah..." By the way Jeff was hemming and hawing, Jason felt something was off. "Jeff, what's up? You have something to tell me?" The day no longer felt so sunny and bright, as he waited for Jeff to get the words out.

Jeff mumbled something about the tomatoes and then took a sharp breath. "Oliver and I didn't know what to do here. But we talked about it this morning and thought it best to say something. It's like we don't want to be holding secrets between us. We've been friends for a long time." He looked at Jason.

"We ran into Mac a couple of times at Leon's bar."

Jason felt confused. "Leon's? When?"

"It was after work. I figured he was out with his crew."

"But," Jason began, shaking his head, "Mac stopped going out to the bars after work. That's what he told me. When would he have gone there?"

Jeff plowed ahead. "You probably noticed his drinking has been getting worse. Well, the other night, I noticed he was with one of the guys who was an actor on some TV show that everyone seems to be watching. Then, a week later, Oliver mentioned that he saw that same actor, Billy Mitchell, with Mac. He asked if you guys were *having trouble."*

Jason found himself getting dizzy and sat down.

"Oliver said it was strange that we kept running into Mac with this actor. And then two weeks ago, we ran into Mac on Fire Island with Billy."

This didn't make sense to Jason. "Two weeks ago?"

"Yeah, so when Billy went to get some more drinks, we asked Mac where you were. He said you were visiting your friends in Vermont, but he looked uncomfortable. He was three sheets to the wind."

Jason couldn't believe what he was hearing. He'd asked Mac to go with him to see the musical, but he'd said he had work. "He was on Fire Island?"

"So, when you were telling us about that show last night, we realized it was the weekend we had seen Mac and Billy on Fire Island. We didn't know what we should do. Oliver and I decided that I should come over and talk to you."

Jason picked up some tomatoes and studied them while he thought of what to say. "Are you sure about all of this?"

They heard the crunch of the gravel outside as Mac's car pulled in the driveway. Jeff said, "I think I better slip out the front. Let's talk later."

Jason tried to push down his anger and surprise. He had started to face Mac's problems with substance use, but this kind of deception was a whole other matter.

Mac burst through the back door and cheerfully announced that he picked up lots of tomatoes, when he noticed the basket on the counter. "Was someone here?"

Jason began to straighten up the kitchen. He kept telling himself that the best thing to do was to stay calm. He knew that Mac would get defensive if he confronted him. He wasn't ready to tell him about the conversation he had with Jeff. He needed to calm down and make sense of what he was feeling. If he gave him a chance, maybe Mac would tell him about Fire Island. He knew he couldn't risk losing his temper.

"So..." Jason started. "That night I had tickets to the show? You said you went to see your mother in Queens. You never said how she was."

Mac pointed to the basket on the counter. "Great tomatoes. Who grew them?"

Jason grasped for an answer. "Sally, from next door." He went over to scour the sink.

"What's wrong?" Mac asked, as he put the produce from the farmers market in the refrigerator. When Jason didn't answer, he turned around and looked at him. "Do you have a hangover? What is it?"

Jason shook his head. "Mac, were you on Fire Island two weeks ago?"

Mac became flushed; he looked sheepish and surprised. A weird expression came over his face. "Look, the business is taking so much out of me, and I didn't want to have to explain or justify that I needed a break."

"So, you didn't tell me that you didn't go to Queens? Who did you go to Fire Island with?"

Mac started to look annoyed. "You are blowing everything out of proportion. We have a lot going on. I don't have time to report every little thing."

"Mac, are you serious?"

"Look, my old friend Billy was in town. I told you about him. We were having drinks, and some people were headed out to Fire Island, and Billy convinced me to come along. I knew you had to stay in the city, and I didn't want to have to explain."

"Mac, you didn't say anything to me about drinks or Billy being here. Come on..."

Jason was feeling a dark cloud pass over his thoughts and just wanted to get out of the room and have some time to think. The story didn't sound right. Mac was stumbling over his words, and it didn't make sense. The back and forth continued as Jason thought Mac looked *more and more desperate. Jason kept busy by cleaning up and reminded himself to stay calm, that this was the best way of handling Mac when he was upset.*

Mac finally admitted, "All right, I've screwed up a few times, but people kept buying me drinks, and I could hardly remember after a certain point. "

"Mac, that's called a blackout. It's not something that most people do on a regular basis. At least not functional people."

"Come on Jason, you know how much pressure this business is. So, I don't make good choices when I've had too much to drink. Nothing terrible happened. I've been cutting down, and I will get it under control."

"What? Are you out of your mind?" He couldn't believe Mac was trying to brush it off. "You think I'm okay with this? Call it an unfortunate incident, and it all goes away?"

"Jason, just tell me what you want," he pleaded. "I'll go to therapy or AA."

"Mac, what I hear is just a whole lot of denial. I have to have some time alone. I'm going back to the city to sort some things out." Jason stormed to the bedroom and began throwing his things into a bag. At this point he realized he, too, had had too much to drank the night before, and he struggled to consider the best way to control the explosion in his head.

He questioned Mac's ability to be honest at this point. Mac's alcohol use had definitely contributed to all of his acting out. Things would not get better until Mac dealt with his drinking issues. He turned to look at Mac, who hovered in the doorway. "Look, let's discuss this when we are both feeling better."

Jason ran out to the car and drove to the city.

Acknowledging, validating, and demonstrating awareness of the impact of one's actions on one's partner is just the first step. It is not only crucial to the process but it must also deepen and expand over time.

"Truth is like the sun. You can shut it out for a time, but it ain't goin' away."

ELVIS PRESLEY

CHAPTER SEVEN

—STEP 2—
BE HONEST

PART OF ACCOUNTABILITY is the willingness to come clean. That means meeting the hurt partner's initial conditions and providing the information they request. You can't be accountable for what you don't admit.

The hurt partner can't fully engage in the repair process without knowing the truth. A formal disclosure process is the most effective way to deal with the hurt partner's need for information. Intense grief and trauma may accompany the disclosure, but the process can mark a significant and positive turning point for many couples.

A formal disclosure process is a defining moment for a life of honesty. In this meeting between the healing and the hurt partners, the healing partner confesses incidents of betrayal, sexual or otherwise, and answers questions that the hurt partner has prepared. Getting through the disclosure process is the first step in creating the transparency required to rebuild trust in the relationship. It shows respect for the hurt partner's need to make sense out of incomprehensible information. It doesn't put them on any kind of solid ground—that can't come until much later—but a formal disclosure does provide an island of sanity amid waves of confusion. In the best cases, it draws a bright line between untruths and truth. The most successful results happen when both partners diligently prepare and work with a specialist to facilitate the disclosure process so that it goes as smoothly and safely as possible.

For the healing partner, it may be challenging to reveal the whole truth all at once. Feelings of guilt and shame, not to mention the fear of causing additional pain to one's partner, might make it seem better to disclose only selected details and still hide the full scope and nature of one's behaviors and feelings. But the hurt partner needs to know the truth in order to heal. Otherwise, they will feel a constant threat of being blindsided. As difficult as these revelations will be for both partners, trust cannot build until all secret doors are opened.

When the hurt partner first discovers the betrayal, there may be a forced or initial disclosure where the acting-out partner reveals parts of the story. However, the whole truth rarely comes out with the initial confrontation after any sort of betrayal. These partial disclosures are often attempts at damage control, an effort to calm the chaos. Most likely, the revelations at this point are only fragments of a much more profound betrayal.

A formal disclosure demonstrates the healing partner's willingness to walk through fire for redemption; it's a sign of accountability and respect for what their partner needs for the repair process to continue. The healing partner's willingness to go through the humiliation and shame of admitting the full extent of their betraying behaviors is a sign of the commitment to healing the relationship.

For an intimate and healthy relationship, the connection must be safe enough to support vulnerable, open, and loving behaviors. This isn't possible when one keeps parts of oneself locked away or when there is a constant threat of your world exploding. When the deceiving partner can't come clean about their lies, secrets, and hidden behaviors, then ongoing ruptures and blowups are inevitable. As Shakespeare famously wrote, "The truth will out." The hurt partner will continually seek information to soothe their anxiety about shadows they fear are still lurking. Once a partner becomes aware of problems with honesty, they'll be hyper-alert to any inconsistencies, and they'll focus on discovering the truth. Their attempts to keep filling in the blanks will fuel increasing conflict, which often unintentionally undermines the repair process.

Secrets and lies create an unequal playing field in which the hurt partner is in a one-down position by not knowing everything that happened and how the healing partner truly feels. Getting through the period after disclosure is very challenging, and both partners need a lot of support to weather the intensity and pain, the shame and anger that will fill the space between them.

A disclosure process is a meeting between the healing and the hurt partners in which the healing partner admits to incidents of betrayal and answers questions that the hurt partner has prepared. It's usually facilitated by a therapist, and in-depth preparation is necessary for the best outcome.

The continuation of Ryan's and Mai's story conveys what a formal disclosure is like. In the first part of their story, Mai, as the hurt partner, was overwhelmed by emotions as she discovered, through bank withdrawals, credit card receipts, and texts that Ryan had been using escort services and acting out sexually. She asked him to leave immediately, and he ended up staying in a room in their basement.

Mai and Ryan (Part 2)

Both Mai and Ryan were still feeling traumatized. Ryan told Mai he would do anything she needed to repair the hurt and pain she felt after discovering his secret life and his acting out. Mai said she was so shaken she couldn't entertain the concept of a future, but if they had any chance of repairing their marriage, he would need to attend therapy with someone who specialized in working with problematic sexual behaviors.

After locating a therapist in their community, Ryan began weekly individual sessions. The therapist also led a men's group for others in recovery from similar issues, and he encouraged Ryan to attend.

Ryan was nervous about the idea of attending a group and talking about all of the shame and fear that he struggled with every day. But after a few meetings he was grateful for how the group helped him feel grounded and gave him a sense of safety when his world felt like it was falling apart. Ryan asked himself how he could have let this happen. He thought of how he had gradually made decisions that he knew were wrong. He would push the incident out of his mind, telling himself it was the last time, but it never was, and the days turned into years.

Ryan felt desperate. He told Mai that he would do

anything to repair the hurt and damage he had done.

Mai said she didn't understand how he could have been so deceitful for so long. At times she felt she couldn't control her rage, that everything in their relationship had been a lie. Her therapist and her women's group became her lifeline, encouraging her to practice the coping strategies she was learning. They supported her need for Ryan to do a formal disclosure as soon as possible. Mai had to know the truth if she was going to make any decisions regarding their future.

The men in Ryan's group had discussed the disclosure process, and his therapist provided worksheets that he could complete to structure the disclosure. Hearing the stories of other men whose relationships were healing after disclosure gave him hope. He thought that he and Mai might be able to get through this difficult but necessary step without separating.

Mai gave him a list of questions that she wanted him to answer in his disclosure letter, in addition to all of the information he had prepared. Ryan worked closely with his therapist to prepare what he was going to read to Mai in the disclosure.

Their disclosure was held in Mai's therapist's office. When Ryan and his therapist arrived, the atmosphere was solemn, and he could feel the tension in the room. Mai listened calmly as Ryan read his disclosure. As he was reading, his voice started to shake. After reading a few pages, his eyes started tearing up, and he choked out a request to stop for a few minutes.

They took a break, and Mai said she wanted to sit in the empty office next door by herself for a few moments to gain her composure. When she returned, she kept her eyes focused on the floor, her face blank and void of emotion. When Ryan finished his disclosure, Mai asked questions in an unemotional tone. Despite the fact that Ryan had admitted to many of his actions in the month prior to their disclosure, the impact of hearing everything again was devastating to Mai. As part of her boundaries and self-care, she had arranged for her sister to pick her up after the disclosure and stay with her that night so that she could have time to process the information.

The next few weeks proved very difficult for both of Ryan and Mai. Ryan attended meetings for compulsive sexual behavior as well as his sexual recovery group. He also stayed committed to attending weekly individual therapy. Ryan's therapist told him that the guilt and shame he felt was an indication that he was doing less compartmentalizing and denial of his actions. Mai depended on her group for ongoing support and sometimes needed to reach out to the other women who were available when the pain became too intense. She appreciated the other group members for listening to her and helping her put all of her overwhelming feelings into words.

"We do what we are and we are what we do."
ABRAHAM MASLOW

CHAPTER EIGHT

—*STEP 3*—
CREATE AGREEMENTS

MAKING AND KEEPING agreements is one of the most effective trust-building behaviors. In many relationships, agreements are unspoken, implicit contracts that govern the couple's expectations of one another. Betrayal throws those expectations to the wind. And when that happens, agreements need to become explicit.

At the beginning of the repair process, the person who betrayed the relationship needs to be clear about their intentions. Do they genuinely want to repair the relationship or merely calm the immediate upset? These intentions need to be clarified with specific agreements that provide their partner with predictability and reassurance about what they can expect. For example, can they agree to cut off contact with the affair partner, stop other acting-out behaviors, and commit to repairing the relationship? If they cannot, then there is no place else to go.

All couples experience degrees of difficulty with assumptions and expectations. Some manage to navigate the delicate dance of nonverbal cues and behavioral norms without too much difficulty. But as Vicki Tidwell Palmer points out in her book on boundaries, *Moving Beyond Betrayal,* an expectation is not an agreement. For relationships damaged by betrayal, expectations need to be clearly defined for the future.

In a relationship where there has been a betrayal, agreements fall into two broad categories: behaviors the healing partner commits to stopping, and behaviors they agree to start. Agreements for new behaviors can be for specific, discrete commitments, such as a daily or weekly check-in. They can be commitments for handling triggering situations in a more effective way. Or they may be about validating agreements with concrete evidence of follow-through with specific plans for ongoing transparency. You can base the content of the agreements on the behavior changes you need to move forward. The important point is that there is clarity about the agreement between the partners. Putting an agreement in writing can help prevent misunderstanding. The hurt partner will be evaluating the trustworthiness of the healing partner by observing the follow-through of the newly clarified agreements.

The healing partner needs to gauge how the hurt partner is experiencing these efforts. Inconsistency with agreements after betrayal will have the effect of negating trust and derailing the repair process. Once you've weathered the initial crisis, you might think the problem is solved. Don't be fooled. Differences and old habits often gradually creep back. Little by little, cracks will appear. The problem may start with arguments over transparency. A request may be ignored. There may be apologies and promises about future behavior. There may be defensive strategies, like cross-complaining, keeping score, or simply stonewalling. In any case, if there is a lack of clarity or transparency, or problems with follow-through, the recovery of trust will be halted.

WALLS AND WINDOWS

In a betrayal, one of you crossed the line—but which line? While everyone understands the definition of the word "boundary," it's often surprising how clueless people can be about the term when it comes to their relationships. Is it okay to have lunch every day of the week with a coworker one is attracted to and confide intimate details about your relationship with your partner? Uh, no. You might not have known it at the time; otherwise, maybe you wouldn't have done it, but that's a boundary violation.

When there is an emotional betrayal, there is a displacement of "walls and windows," as Shirley Glass explains in her classic book, *Not Just Friends*. She notes that betrayal begins with the construction of walls. These are built slowly, brick by brick. It can start with a simple lie of omission, not mentioning people, places, and things that you know your partner would question or have a problem with. At first you rationalize that it's better not to upset your partner over a single incident. But then the events turn into patterns, and the narrative of why this wall is a good idea expands with the placement of each brick concealing more and more of who you are. Suddenly there is a whole room of your life where you live out a part of you in a role that your partner doesn't even know exits.

Other people, however, are visiting those hidden rooms and spending time there. They have access to essential parts of you that you rationalize, deny, and compartmentalize when you can. And this visiting cast of characters starts to know more about who you are and where you are going than your partner. You both need to agree on restructuring the wall of secrets and lies and opening up windows of transparency.

TRANSPARENCY TO VALIDATE AGREEMENTS

As you begin to forge new agreements, honesty and transparency in the relationship (past, present, and future) become paramount. A disclosure is the start of providing ongoing transparency that demonstrates the healing partner's commitment to repairing trust. Because of the severity of the deception, however, there needs to be an ongoing series of mutual agreements that clarify expectations about transparency.

There will be specific transparency needs for each couple, depending on the nature of the hidden information and areas where the hurt partner needs reassurance. Is your partner afraid that you will lie about who you are with or what you are doing on your computer? Depending on what your partner is concerned about, this might include providing email passwords, allowing your partner access to your phone's location information, or only using a computer when your partner is present. It might mean making sure your partner can monitor financial transactions. Sometimes it might require something as extreme as changing jobs. These actions are part of doing whatever it takes to reassure your partner and help them manage the anxieties and fears that will be present for some time.

When you withhold information from your partner because you think it could lead to conflict, you are giving yourself permission to position the walls and windows in your relationship in a way that's convenient for you. But this behavior is also destructive to building trust. Repair is about increasing your tolerance for difficult emotions and challenging situations that are necessary not just for repair but for a strong intimate relationship.

In the following story, stonewalling and a lack of transparency erode the trust in a couple's relationship.

Kelly and Ugo (Part 1)

Kelly had been attending a women's support group, trying to learn coping strategies to deal with her anxieties about her relationship with Ugo. Kelly said whenever she tried to talk to Ugo about their lack of connection he would either get angry and defensive or walk away, leaving whatever room they were in and slamming the door behind him.

"We don't have sex anymore," she said. "It seems that we fight all the time, and we are locked in a power struggle about who's to blame when we fight. If I try to talk to him about people he's spending time with and I ask to meet, he always makes some excuse. He said that he works hard so that I don't have to work right now, so I can focus my time and attention on raising our son. I know I should be grateful that he works so hard, but I don't understand why he has to work until midnight so many days a week. Sometimes I get so upset I wake

him in the middle of the night and ask him what time he got home. He says I'm crazy, and he can't deal with how emotional I am all the time.

"I tried to explain to Ugo that these women he was spending time with were not mutual friends—he kept these relationships separate. It's almost like he has a secret life. I said to him, 'We don't socialize with them. They are not friends of ours as a couple.' Couldn't he understand how that could make me feel insecure about our relationship? He keeps saying that if I don't trust him, we should just call it quits. He said I was making a big deal out of the texts he gets all the time, and I was being paranoid and crazy. He doesn't seem to be willing to work at solving these issues. It's like every day I get my hopes up that these issues will go away, and then I sink back to feeling powerless that anything can change."

A month later Kelly let the group know that she would be missing a few meetings because she and Ugo were going to spend a month in Italy sightseeing and visiting his family. She was excited about the trip and thought it would be a time for them to reconnect and put the conflicts of the past few months behind them.

But a week later she was back. And when she walked into the meeting room, something was clearly wrong. "I thought I would still be in Italy tonight," she said. "But there's no way I could stay. I flew back yesterday after three days.

"The first few days I felt happy for the first time in months. Tuscany is so beautiful in the spring, and I remembered the good times Ugo and I had when we had first met. I had been trying to focus away from what he was doing and started to think that maybe my suspicions were wrong. We were getting along better and even laughing as we drove from Florence to Ugo's parents' house. Tuscany felt like a respite. I thought that maybe all the problems were behind us.

"But then Ugo started to have trouble with directions and asked me to check his phone's GPS. A text message saying, 'I miss you,' popped up on the screen. I went numb and didn't want to react without giving myself a chance to get more information. A part of me almost knew or expected to see something like this at some point. Maybe that's why I never tried to look at his phone. I asked him, 'Why would a female friend say that she misses you after three days?' He must think I'm stupid," Kelly said.

"Right now, I feel that his commitment to the relationship is a minus one," Kelly said. "I guess I need to face this. He thinks that I'm the problem and that's the only thing that needs to change."

She told the group that she wasn't ready to make the next step to establish a bottom line. "I feel like I'm clinging to a sinking ship. Ugo is being untruthful and evasive. I asked for transparency. I asked to see his texts and emails. He said he stopped talking to the woman whose text I saw when we were in Italy. But I think he's lying. Every time he comes home late, I wonder where he was and who he was with. I even considered hiring a private detective."

Ugo complained that Kelly was being controlling by asking to see his texts or emails. She began regularly checking his phone and discovered that he seemed to be erasing all his texts. The next time she tried to check his phone when he was in the shower it was locked.

Her suspicions grew to the point where she could no longer handle it and found herself taking desperate measures, which she described at the next group. "I hid a tape recorder in Ugo's car. I heard him speaking with the woman from the text messages, and the relationship was obviously more than just coworkers. And they are still seeing each other. I felt terrible about myself, sinking to this level of spying. But I realized that I couldn't go on this way."

AGREEMENTS FOR NEW BOUNDARIES

Just as agreements concerning other aspects of behavior need to be made explicit, a couple needs a clear, mutual agreement about the specific boundaries in the relationship, the lines that shouldn't be crossed. Your boundaries tell other people how they can treat you—what behaviors are acceptable and what are not. The boundaries around you and your partner with others on the outside need to be refined with examples of where and when the line around the relationship is crossed.

An example of a boundary agreement is, "I will let you know within 24 hours if the person I was seeing outside our relationship tries to contact me." These clear, time-bound agreements provide safety for the hurt partner who fears discovering another lie or betrayal. They need to feel some certainty that their partner will not lie or deceive them if they are going to have a future together. The healing partner's ability to be honest is a crucial part of rebuilding trust. But as the hurt partner, you still need to move cautiously. Don't take emotional risks until you have developed strong emotional regulation techniques and have established a strong support network.

TOOLS

THREE CIRCLES TOOL

This tool simplifies and defines how behaviors need to be changed. The partners envision an inner, red circle that includes behaviors that both agree are totally off-limits. There is a middle or yellow circle that contains behaviors that lead to the red circle; these need to be avoided. The outer, green circle includes positive behaviors that the partners want to increase and that nurture the connection, support recovery, and enhance relationship repair. The three circles lay out clear examples of the most crucial behaviors changes that are part of establishing transparency, accountability, and trust.

This is an example of a possible three circles diagram.

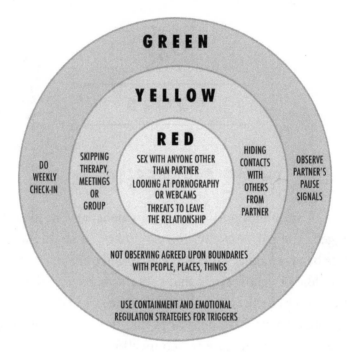

GREEN

YELLOW

RED

DO WEEKLY CHECK-IN

SKIPPING THERAPY, MEETINGS OR GROUP

SEX WITH ANYONE OTHER THAN PARTNER

LOOKING AT PORNOGRAPHY OR WEBCAMS

THREATS TO LEAVE THE RELATIONSHIP

HIDING CONTACTS WITH OTHERS FROM PARTNER

OBSERVE PARTNER'S PAUSE SIGNALS

NOT OBSERVING AGREED UPON BOUNDARIES WITH PEOPLE, PLACES, THINGS

USE CONTAINMENT AND EMOTIONAL REGULATION STRATEGIES FOR TRIGGERS

THE CHECK-IN

This tool goes a long way to building trust and demonstrating the commitment to repair. It includes the following steps:

1. Make an agreement for a regular time to do the check-in.

2. Agree on the components of the check-in (identifying feelings, sobriety time established, needs or concerns, positive or challenging situations you each experienced). Keep the list short.

3. Make the check-in a ritual with a regular schedule.

Blair and Marcus (Part 2)

In his quest to establish new boundaries around his relationship with Blair, Marcus used the Three Circles Tool to define his specific contact with Mariah going forward. She was pushing back, and he struggled with telling Blair about her attempts to contact him, but his group helped him stay honest with himself. He and Blair were still living separately, and he knew he had to take the initiative to discuss all the times Mariah had tried to contact him in the check-ins that he and Blair had agreed to over video chat.

His agreement that he would stop all contact with Mariah was not as easy to manage as he had hoped. Marcus explained to his group how he told Mariah he was committed to his marriage and that he needed to stop spending time with her. But Blair was still anxious, knowing that he and Mariah worked together Marcus worked at providing transparency for Blair by letting her know if Mariah tried to contact him. He proposed that he write an email to Mariah, which he would share with Blair, explaining exactly what he felt, and how he would respond to any attempts Mariah made to contact him.

Blair felt reassured that Marcus was trying to create a stronger boundary with Mariah. Additionally, he made an agreement that he would let Blair know within 24 hours if Mariah tried to contact him, or if they were communicating for any reason.

Marcus was taking down the walls that he had constructed with Blair and closing the windows that were open with Mariah.

Marcus gave Blair the passwords to his accounts and told her that she was free to look at his texts and emails any time she wanted. When Blair noticed that Marcus hadn't initiated a check-in on their usual night, she wondered if there was something wrong. She decided to look at Marcus's emails and saw one from Mariah. She opened it and she saw a message "Why won't you answer my texts?" She elected not to confront Marcus with this but to wait and see if he would mention it. She struggled with the decision about bringing it up.

The next night Marcus contacted Blair and asked to meet for dinner. Blair agreed but did not know what to expect, though as soon as they sat down, Marcus said, "I know I missed the last check-in. I want to be honest about everything and felt conflicted about what to say about this. I didn't want to lie by omission. So I just avoided the check-in while I was trying to figure out how to tell you this.

"Mariah texted me the last two days, and I didn't respond but I know I broke our agreement by not telling you. Then yesterday I found this note in an envelope on my desk. Here, take a look at it."

It was a note from Mariah pleading with Marcus to contact her and asking if they could meet one more time. "Blair, I want us to figure out how to handle this together," Marcus said. He showed Blair a response he could send, and Blair agreed to it. Marcus told Mariah that he would no longer see her and, in fact, was transferring to another beat so they would not be working together anymore.

AGREEMENTS FOR EMOTIONALLY CHARGED MOMENTS

The extreme emotional reactivity of early repair will be challenging for both partners. When there is a high level of emotional conflict some agreements can help. Agreements provide a systemic structure for resolving the immediate conflicts that will arise on a daily basis soon after discovery of a betrayal. The hurt partner will be frequently triggered. Often these situations are confusing for the healing partner, who doesn't know how to respond in an effective and empathic way.

When tempers flare, a mutual agreement of how you will work together to handle these volatile situations can help calm the storm. These agreements work by establishing predictability for inevitable blowups that otherwise might spiral out of control.

For example, if the hurt partner discovered the betrayal through a text message, the ping of a phone alert could trigger anxiety and other painful feelings. With an agreement in place about how to handle such a situation, both partners know what to expect. The agreement would make clear that the healing partner will offer to share the contents of those texts. In that way, the hurt partner doesn't feel blindsided or feel the need to react, and the healing partner doesn't feel blamed or accused.

Even with agreements governing behavior, sometimes interactions can become too heated. In that case, one important agreement is for a pause or time-out. This may be very difficult for the hurt partner to observe in the earliest days of repair. The best strategy for the healing partner is simply responding to their partner, telling them what you hear they are feeling and thinking and asking if you are understanding them correctly.

One of the traps many couples fall into is that the agreements are too vague. They need to be detailed, specific, and time bound. The agreements can't be broken without discussion or negotiation, as this would be a major step backward in repairing trust.

As the repair process proceeds, both partners should be able to initiate the pause tool. It is easiest when the signal that either of you needs this break is very clear and simple, such as a safe word. Any neutral or even humorous word will do.

"If there is no struggle, there is no progress."
FREDERICK DOUGLASS

CHAPTER NINE

—STEP 4—
EVALUATE PROGRESS

I F YOU ARE the hurt partner, you will be evaluating whether the relationship can be repaired as you move through the first steps of this process. At this stage in the healing plan, you can control how much you engage with your partner, as well as the conditions you need for your healing and safety. Don't be fooled by false humility or pressure to quickly put incidents behind you. Differences and old habits often gradually reemerge. You might find yourself making excuses for your partner. Objective support from a therapist or support group can help you face what your partner is willing or not willing to do. Some couples get over the initial crisis, but because trust is not restored they remain at this stage. Their relationship may exist in limbo, with neither partner feeling fulfilled or happy for weeks, months, or even years.

It's important not to blame the process but to be accountable for how it is being executed. In my work with couples who are trying to repair their relationship, if the healing partner is not willing to be accountable for how their actions affect their partner and won't fully commit to following through with each of these steps, the process will fall apart. It will take the hurt partner some time to believe in the process and for trust to build. The hurt partner has a choice to join the process of repair or not. Only the people involved can decide when they have had enough.

Here are some questions that the hurt partner can use to evaluate their situation.

- Do you feel your partner has the willingness to do what it takes to repair the relationship?

- Do you see changes that demonstrate more commitment?

- Are they willing to provide a degree of transparency that you are comfortable with?

- Do you feel that you have to ask for information, or are they willing to provide it?

- Do they respond with defensiveness when you ask a question or make a request?

- Are they working on new skills such as more effective communication?

- Are they keeping agreements?

- Do you feel an increase in your ability to trust your partner?

CONSISTENCY AND FOLLOW-THROUGH

Inconsistency with agreements after betrayal will erode trust and derail the healing process. For example, if daily interactions aren't meeting needs for empathy, communication, or positive connection, frustration and anger can build. The wounded partner will go back to being consumed by the beliefs and feelings from the betrayal, erasing progress. And if the healing partner is ambivalent about the commitment required for repair or expects to get credit for their efforts, the repair will falter.

It's important to understand that progress will come, but usually only after the third or fourth month of consistent and reliable efforts. The first six months will be especially difficult for both partners. Later there will be time to examine longstanding patterns in the relationship. Then the focus can shift to mutuality, where both partner's needs are fully addressed.

Jason and Mac (Part 2)

Despite his feelings of betrayal by Mac, and Mac's unwillingness to be completely accountable for his actions, Jason decided to continue their relationship. He and Mac made some agreements, and Jason started attending a support group. There they discussed the need for boundaries, setting bottom-line conditions, and avoiding making threats. When Jason talked to Mac about doing a disclosure of his sexual behavior, however, Mac said he couldn't do it for another month or two, until after Christmas. He said he needed work to slow down first.

Jason heard stories in the group about the need to be clear and that both partners had choices. He learned how important it was to take care of himself during this process. In the meantime, Jason's doubts about Mac's honesty persisted. He smelled alcohol on Mac several times, and some days Mac wouldn't answer Jason's texts for hours. Jason started to question if he had made the right decision in giving their relationship another chance. He understood that it wasn't easy for Mac to give up alcohol, and he knew that a relapse was more than likely. Nevertheless Jason reassured himself with the agreements that he and Mac had made, including one that Mac would come clean with Jason within 24 hours if there were any slips.

Mac kept pushing back the date of the disclosure. One afternoon, while Mac was in the shower, his phone buzzed. Jason picked it up and began reading the texts, all of them from Mac's old friend Billy. Jason felt himself shutting down inside. It was clear that Mac was still spending time with Billy and lying about it. There was no other explanation or excuse for the messages. He had to face the fact that Mac wasn't ready to make the changes he needed. For his own well-being he knew he had to end the relationship.

THE NEED FOR ONGOING SUPPORT

During the repair process both partners will experience painful emotions, though it is the acting-out partner who must come to terms with what led them to betray their partner in the first place. To do that during the early steps of repair the healing partner needs guidance. Individual therapy is best supported with participation in a group with similar goals. It will provide an experience of acceptance that reduces the feelings of shame that can block the development of self-awareness and insight. Through participating in this group culture, the healing partner will learn to increase their tolerance for uncomfortable feelings and face hard truths as they move out of denial. Facing these feelings requires safety, support, and confidentiality. When there's a bump in the road, participation in a group is a way to keep the process in perspective and clarify thoughts and feelings.

The success of AA is founded on these principles. The human connection replaces the connection with a substance or behavior. When a group of people gathers together in a room, their shared hope and acceptance of each other with all their differences create a palpable energy. It allows us to overcome our egos and align with a higher purpose. We discover a spiritual element whenever we dissolve our separateness, merging safely in unison and moving toward hope and healing. In those moments, we aren't held back. We are no longer focusing on protecting ourselves by closing off and shutting down.

Kelly and Ugo (Part 2)

Kelly decided that she had reached the point where she needed to establish a nonnegotiable boundary and asked Ugo to move out. She told him she felt he was not willing to work on what she needed to repair their relationship.

She felt that he was unresponsive to all of her requests. He didn't show the interest or desire to make changes to the way they communicated. Her therapist suggested a men's support group for Ugo, but he said that he didn't need that and blamed Kelly for the separation. He felt angry and filled with resentment for how Kelly was acting, saying she was trying to control him. But his problems were only just beginning.

The woman Ugo was seeing in his office started making her own demands. She wanted him to move in with her. She was furious when he refused and threatened to go to HR and report their sexual relationship. Ugo wanted to end it, but her threats scared him. Before long, he found himself missing the comforts of home and his life with Kelly and their son, Paolo.

Ugo felt he had made a mess of things, but he couldn't understand why. After losing his temper at work, he decided to try going to the men's group. At the very least, he thought it might give him a place to vent his anger so he could keep his cool when he really needed to. As he listened to the stories and resentments of other men in similar situations to his own, however, he began to see himself in their predicaments.

The group turned out to be a lifeline for Ugo. A few weeks after he started attending, he was let go from his job. The company told him they were eliminating his position, but he wondered if the woman he had been involved with had played any role in what happened. He continued to attend the group and felt less alone in trying to manage his anger.

One evening the group did an exercise where they listed their problems, secrets, and excuses. The other men's lists sounded uncomfortably familiar to Ugo, and he started to see the role that he had played in creating problems in his life. When he read his own list to his group, he felt ashamed. As he learned more about how the men were working at repairing their lives and relationships, Ugo came to realize that he had believed Kelly would have a problem with him no matter what he did. He decided he would try to work things out with Kelly. He also realized he needed help.

"Words can sometimes, in moments of grace,
attain the quality of deeds."
ELIE WIESEL

CHAPTER TEN

—*STEP 5*—
IMPROVE ATTUNEMENT
AND EMPATHY

A TTUNEMENT is reacting to another's emotional state in a way that they feel understood and valued. It's establishing a good emotional connection, becoming aware of and meeting your mate's needs for empathy, understanding, or reassurance in day-to-day interactions. Wouldn't it be great if you could anticipate the needs of your partner before they get hurt or angry? That's what's known as having good attunement. These repair steps can develop trust, but other skills and actions are needed to create the emotional connection that has to accompany repair. Attunement is established when you are able to recognize a need in your partner and to respond with comfort and reassurance. The key is to recognize what John Gottman terms your partner's "bids"—how they communicate what they need to feel connected—by being emotionally reliable at these critical moments and by responding in a caring way.

John Gottman, the author of *Why Marriages Succeed*, explains that bids are times when a partner wants attention, though these may not be expressed directly or verbally. Some couples consistently fail to understand each other's bids; they are on two separate wavelengths and are in constant conflict as a result. But arguments and misunderstandings aren't the only factors in frayed relationships. Many other relationships break down because of neglect. Turning away from your partner's bids is what really corrodes the connection, according to Gottman. That is why improving attunement and empathy are the next step in repairing a relationship.

Attunement is a key part of the empathy that's needed to repair the emotional connection. It's when you are able to recognize a need in your partner and to respond with comfort and reassurance. It's a learning process, as is each one of these steps. As these new behaviors and ways of thinking become embedded as habits in your relationship, you will notice that life becomes easier

This is where partners' connection begins to change. But it's also where many relationships get stalled. Attunement lays the foundations for the kind of intimacy and connection the couple will create together. It requires that both parties show interest and curiosity. And unless there is *genuine* interest, attunement is hard to achieve. One of the biggest problems in couples' relationships is when a need goes unrecognized or is not understood due to a failure in communication, interest, or attunement.

Good communication skills can help bridge the gap, and we'll address that further in Step Six. However, if you are clueless about the needs behind your partner's requests, then attunement will always be out of reach. Repair and healing happen in daily, seemingly trivial interactions. By hearing your partner's bids—identifying the possibility of a misunderstanding and resolving it before it becomes something bigger—you are building trust and your emotional connection. This means picking up on what your partner is experiencing and responding in a way that makes them feel acknowledged and cared for.

John Gottman has outlined some simple steps to improve attunement:

1. Put your feelings into words.

2. Ask open-ended questions.

3. Follow up with statements that deepen the connection.

4. Give empathy, not advice.

Effective communication is not just informing your partner about something that was hurtful in the moment. It's giving them the information they need to develop more awareness and understanding about the relationship. The hurt partner needs to say what is needed when nonverbal cues go unrecognized. The healing partner has to respond to their partner in a way that makes them feel heard and understood. Honesty is essential, but it's not enough. The healing partner has to take the initiative, communicating in daily interactions and addressing larger concerns in an effective yet compassionate and nondestructive manner.

The dialogue process, or reflective listening, offers a way to learn to communicate effectively. Harville Hendrix, the originator of the process, teaches a specific format that eliminates any power struggle and keeps one partner from hijacking the conversation back to their concerns. Taking turns prevents the breakdown of communication and the escalation of anger and frustration.

Here's a summary of the process:

DIALOGUE STEPS FOR SENDER

1. Ask your partner for time to express your concern. (They should give you a time that works for them.)

2. Express your concern briefly with no blame or criticism.

3. After your partner mirrors your concern, let them know if they got it.

DIALOGUE STEPS FOR RECEIVER

1. Mirror. Summarize your partner's concern. Ask if you got it; if they say no, ask them to repeat it and try again to mirror their concern.

2. Validate. Tell them what makes sense about this concern. This does not mean you agree. It means you can understand their feelings from their perspective. This demonstration of empathy will go a long way to smoothing disagreements, healing ruptures, and strengthening your relationship.

3. Optional Step. Ask your partner what they think will help with the resolution of the concern. Ask for one way that you might meet an immediate need that is causing distress. What action could have a positive effect?

4. It helps to practice using the dialogue skill, which can be difficult and frustrating at first. Start with smaller concerns. It gets easier and more effective the more you learn to use it.

Mai and Ryan (Part 3)

As the months passed, Mai felt less triggered on a daily basis. Ryan had worked through the steps of the repair process with the help of his therapist and group—accountability, transparency, making explicit agreements with follow-up, and using tools like the three circles and check-ins. They were hitting the one-year mark after Mai had felt her world crash. Now they were co-existing peacefully, but Mai still felt that the connection she needed was missing. They started attending weekly couples sessions. Mai said that she didn't feel empathy from Ryan in how he responded to her. She said that she didn't feel like he heard her; it seemed like he was only reacting to what was in his head, responding the way he felt he was supposed to do.

They were introduced to the dialogue process and asked to try it in the therapist's office. The advantage of the dialogue is that it slows down the automatic respond-and-react nature of typical conversations. Mirroring and validating a partner's response show that one is attentive and listening.

Using this process, Mai was encouraged to voice her feelings as concerns. Both she and Ryan needed to learn to take steps to get past difficult moments and use the opportunity to create connection. If they got stuck in the belief that nothing could change, then it certainly would not.

Ryan explained that the things he did to help Mai feel better seemed to backfire. "I'm not sure if she's angry at the whole situation or at something I just did. I want to do the right thing, but sometimes I just don't know what that is."

"Do you ask Mai for a time when she would be open to discussing what happened and try to express your concern with the dialogue?" their therapist asked. Ryan admitted they had only tried it once.

During the next couple of sessions, the couple focused on developing this communication tool. The attunement in their relationship had been broken for some time, and they each needed to each learn how to improve it. It was important for them to continue translating any negative feelings into concerns without criticism or blame. By using the dialogue, they would gain the skills to approach difficult topics. But it was crucial they ask for a time first, rather than just blindside each other.

RYAN AND MAI'S DIALOGUE

Ryan: *Mai, are you available to do a dialogue now? Thanks for making yourself available.*

Mai: *Yes, we can do it now.*

Ryan: *I'm concerned that when I got home from my group last night, you seemed annoyed with me. I'm wondering if I did something to upset you yesterday, or was it from things that have happened before? If I know what's upsetting you, I can try to do something about it. I really want to understand what's wrong.*

Mai: *Sometimes I feel like you just don't listen or pay attention.*

Therapist: *Mai, before you tell Ryan why you were annoyed, you want to establish a connection by making sure that he feels heard. Let's start by making sure that Ryan feels heard by mirroring and validating his concern.*

Mai: *"So, Ryan, you're concerned that I was angry at you for something yesterday. You want to know if I was thinking about the past or if I was annoyed at something you did yesterday. Did I get it?"*

Ryan: *"Yes. I would really like you to tell me when something I'm doing is bothering you."*

Mai: *"It makes sense that you want to understand why I'm upset."*

Therapist: *"It's important to stay with one person's concern at a time and not cross complain. But I'm going to ask you to switch roles now for the sake of practicing and so you both have a chance to express a concern. Mai, why don't you express your concern to Ryan about him not paying attention."*

Mai: *"Ryan, you did read the situation correctly. I was annoyed at you. I had asked if you would pick up some coffee for tomorrow, and you came home without it. You completely forgot. Then I started to think about how you weren't paying attention all those years when I was saying that I thought we had a problem in our relationship. And you couldn't be honest. I just kept trying to figure out what was wrong. I felt like I was doing all the work. I don't want to feel that way anymore.*

Ryan: *So let me make sure I've got it. You were disappointed and upset when I came home and hadn't done what you had requested. I acted like I didn't even remember that you had asked me to get coffee for tomorrow morning. And that brought up thoughts about how*

127

shut down I was in the past and how you kept trying to fix things, and I wasn't able to admit how screwed up I was. Did I get it?

Mai: *Most of it.*

Ryan: *Let me try a bit more. So, you started to feel really alone, remembering how hard you tried, and I didn't meet you halfway. And worse, I lied about my hurtful behaviors, covering them up for a long time. You worked hard at our relationship, and I didn't, and you don't want to go back to that place again. Did I get it all?*

Mai: *I think so.*

Ryan: *It makes sense that you would feel hurt when you make a simple request, and I don't observe it, or I act like I am not paying attention to something important to you. It makes sense that you would feel that you are always the one that has to carry the relationship, and you're tired of doing that. You would like me to be more active and work harder at trying to understand what's important to you and to follow through. It makes sense that what I say isn't as important as showing you that you are important to me.*

Mai remains silent.

Ryan: *Is there more you would like to say?*

Mai: *No.*

Therapist: *Ryan, is there anything else you would like to say.*

Ryan: *Yes. I'm so sorry, Mai. I know I've let you down over and over and have caused so much pain to you and to our family. I will spend the rest of my life trying to make it up. I appreciate you telling me how you feel. I want to hear whenever you feel disappointed or upset."*

Therapist: *Understanding what's important to your*

partner and having the curiosity to keep learning to read each other's needs is the beginning of attaining good attunement. Mai, would you like to express a concern?

Mai: *(Quiet, on the verge of tears) I don't know if this can ever be different. I'm just tired of trying.*

Ryan: *(Reaching out for her hand) I am so sorry. I will try harder.*

Ryan started to understand how he had put up walls when he felt uncomfortable. This blocked him from receiving the information he needed to make the right choices. Their therapist emphasized the need for them to shift into the dialogue process so they could learn more about what each needed and how to respond in a way that increased communication and connection. It was important for Ryan to learn about the hurt behind Mai's anger.

"Ryan, try to move past the belief that there is nothing you can do or that you have to give Mai a solution to her feelings," the therapist said. "For the connection to start, you have to show her that you understand and have empathy for what she's feeling."

Empathy is an active process. It's demonstrated when you provide comfort or reassurance. Attunement is a key part of empathy. It's being able to recognize a need in your partner and to respond to it in a healing way. It's demonstrated in your readiness and willingness to respond with compassion when your partner is triggered. It's a learning process, as is each one of these steps.

Dr. Rob Weiss' *Out of the Doghouse, A Step-By-Step Relationship-Saving Guide for Men Caught Cheating*, is an excellent resource for improving your ability to be empathic. In clear and straightforward prose, he paints a realistic picture of what is needed in the early days of relationship repair when the hurt partner is still in an extremely fragile and reactive state. "This is a book written for heterosexual men who have cheated on a woman they love, have gotten caught, and don't want to lose their relationship with her," says Dr. Weiss. Learning how to respond to your partner in critical moments with empathy and compassion is a key part of the repair process.

The following questions will help you assess the attunement and empathy you feel with your partner.

QUESTIONS FOR REFLECTION FOR THE HURT PARTNER

- Is your partner interested in your thoughts and feelings?

- Is your partner empathetic and understanding about your needs for transparency to rebuild the damaged trust?

- Do you see an increase in self-awareness?

- Does your partner validate and respond with understanding to your feelings?

QUESTIONS FOR REFLECTION
FOR THE HEALING PARTNER

- Do you show interest in what your partner is expressing?

- How can you soothe your partner's distress and stay connected?

- Do you feel that you check out sometimes?

- What emotions do you feel when you check out?

"The single biggest problem in communication is the illusion that it has taken place."
GEORGE BERNARD SHAW

CHAPTER ELEVEN

—STEP 6—
LEARN COMMUNICATION AND CONFLICT-REPAIR SKILLS

A FTER THE INITIAL storm passes, you might think everything will be smooth sailing. But every couple in a relationship will experience conflicts and differences that can escalate. The important thing to realize is that you both need a plan and an agreement for how you will handle those issues when they occur.

You need to come to a mutual commitment and understanding so conflict isn't a zero-sum game. You need to avoid what psychologist Pia Mellody calls going "one up," when you position yourself as the one who's right and the other is wrong. Old habits can gradually creep back. As we've pointed out, you need to follow through and maintain consistency for the repair plan to work. This is often the most difficult part of the process.

Learning conflict-repair skills and having an agreement on how you will handle the inevitable conflicts that are part of any long-term relationship will give you the confidence to take effective actions. You won't retreat and ignore ruptures that can fester and grow larger over time. Conflict avoidance leads to bigger problems. When you notice the start of a potential conflict, you can take a proactive approach by asking for time to address a concern. Use the dialogue process to further your understanding of what the real issues are.

When you use the dialogue technique, you are addressing two parts of the conflict—the material content and the emotional aspect. In the first part of the dialogue, you are learning how your partner sees the issue and, by implication, get a clue to what they might need and feel. When you add a sentence that validates their perceptions, you are addressing how your partner feels in a way that they won't feel judged or worry that you are going one-up on them. For example, a rather typical argument about who loads the dishwasher or takes out the trash is also about feeling valued and not taken for granted. Both parts of the equation need to be addressed.

When you get to a good place with the repair process, you will need to give your partner the benefit of the doubt and have faith and hope that you will be able to resolve difficult issues with mutual respect. You will both need the discipline, interest, and skills to effectively identify the nature and components of the rupture and use appropriate conflict resolution techniques.

Only when you have learned to use the dialogue process fluently will you be able to experience its power. You will see how anger and anxiety drain away. You will see how you can sweep over a potential conflict, spread calm, and find a way to resolution. But you have to make an agreement to use it and have the commitment to make it a habit. The dialogue process requires that you have enough interest in your partner to want to understand their position. It offers opportunities to further your healing and connection.

Carrie and Mick

Carrie and Mick had no tools to resolve a conflict without it turning into an epic battle. Mick liked order and calm, but he was attracted to the excitement of Carrie's emotional personality. Looking at pornography had been something he relied on for escape when he felt overwhelmed by stress at work or from arguments with Carrie. Lately, he felt that he was turning to it more and more, feeling the need for a greater fix.

"When Carrie looked at my browser history," he said, "she flew into a rage and started throwing things at me, including my laptop. It was frightening, but in a weird way, it made me feel justified in my actions. I felt she had no right to be so abusive just because I had looked at porn.

"I told myself that I was a good provider. I made enough money so that she could go back to school. I had not really been unfaithful—and she was completely overreacting.

"Just to keep the peace, I promised that I would stop looking at porn. Instead, I began to go on webcams and watch live sex while I masturbated. Probably not the smartest thing in the world to do, but I wasn't exactly thinking clearly. Of course, she found out again. I suggested that we see a counselor. The counselor had us

draw up a three circles agreement. We agreed to use a safe word if either of us was noticing that our emotions were getting to a dangerous point."

MICK AND CARRIE'S THREE CIRCLES AGREEMENT

RED—UNACCEPTABLE BEHAVIORS

No sex with anyone other than partner

No looking at pornography or webcams

No yelling or extreme expressions of anger

No threats to leave the relationship

No throwing things at partner

Do not block partner if they need to leave for a break

YELLOW—CAUTION —LEADS TO RED CIRCLE

Don't discuss relationship with partner with others except group/therapist

Don't stonewall when Carrie asks questions

Provide open access to texts and emails

Don't communicate with blame or criticism

Don't tell partner how to do something or criticize how they are handling something

GREEN—DO MORE OF THESE

Do weekly check-in

Be open about current challenges with the recovery process

Attend support groups weekly

Have strategies to deal with situations that trigger anger or other strong emotions

Identify ongoing relationship frustrations

Use dialogue process when having a relationship concern

Observe partner's pause signals

Ask partner for time to express concern if feeling triggered

Learn containment and emotional regulation strategies for triggers

"I can see that Carrie has a lot of anger toward me," Mick went on. "She says that she feels I'm trying to control her and always telling her what to do. I understand that her father was very rigid and controlling and had a very bad temper. I know she had a lot of trauma in her childhood from the constant fighting between her parents. A big part of that was her father being dishonest with her mother.

"I realized that maybe we were re-enacting some childhood drama of hers and maybe mine, too. I knew if I didn't stop these behaviors, we would stay in this destructive cycle. But I also needed to show Carrie that I was changing. We worked out some agreements where I would only use the computer in the living room with my screen where she could see it. I agreed to attend a men's group for sexually compulsive behavior. Carrie agreed to attend an anger-management group.

"We have had some good weeks. We have a ritual of going out for lunch every Saturday, and we have a safe word we use when one of us feels that we're going to start yelling or get really angry. We take a break and come back to the conversation and use the dialogue process. It's getting easier. I really want this relationship to work out."

Sometimes your partner won't immediately know why they're upset. This isn't the time to give up. It's an opportunity to build a reliable connection. Begin by taking the initiative to let your partner know you want to understand their feelings. Often there is a huge hesitancy to ask for more information about what your mate needs. But this sends a message about a lack of interest.

Instead, being attuned and showing empathy—letting your partner know that they are heard and understood—will often solve a large portion of the issue. For either partner, withdrawing and running for cover is the worst thing you can do. If you believe your partner is going to find a problem with you no matter what, that belief becomes a big problem in and of itself.

Good communication also involves knowing how to express routine exchanges in a clear and effective way. There's a difference between a request and a demand. Requests are asking for your partner to willingly meet a certain need. How your mate responds to the request and how they follow through will give you important information about the seriousness of their commitment to repairing the relationship. When you frame your concern as a demand, your partner may agree just to try to calm the conflict. There may be a begrudging half-compliance that backfires and creates disappointment and resentment in their partner.

Mai and Ryan (Part 4)

Mai and Ryan continued to use the dialogue process to improve their communication over concerns. After several months Mai reported that Ryan's way of responding had made a big difference.

"It helped a lot for me to understand and really listen to the things that Mai wanted from me," said Ryan. "Listening wasn't something I did very well. I was stuck inside my own head. I used to dismiss her concern as unfair because it wasn't the way I thought about it. I thought she was making a big deal out of nothing," he said. "But I see that the point is larger than what we are arguing about in the moment—it's about us getting on the same wavelength by treating each other's feelings and thoughts with respect."

As Ryan learned to listen and acknowledge that Mai's feelings made sense, she started to feel more and more relief and less buildup of anger. They started to find that they could talk without growing emotional, and Ryan would initiate a check-in that made Mai feel his interest and caring. As they headed into the third year of the recovery process, they each felt more confident in their ability to handle the challenges that would emerge and the feelings that went with them.

Mai also began to see their past interactions in a new light.

"I can see now that we really didn't have the skills to talk to each other about what we each needed," she said. "I had this assumption that he should be able to read my mind about what was important to me. And then we would each just react—me with criticizing and Ryan by withdrawing. We each felt like we were the victim of the other person's actions, instead of looking at what we could do to communicate and really understand each other.

"At first, Ryan would buy me chocolate as a way of trying to make up for what he did or when I was angry," she said. "But that didn't make me feel better. It wasn't what I wanted, and I felt like he didn't care enough to try to understand what was wrong."

Mai started to give Ryan suggestions about things that would make her feel cared for. "Now," she said, "he isn't withdrawing. I'm starting to feel that he's more reliable and interested in understanding where I'm coming from. He is paying attention," she said smiling at Ryan, "which is way better than chocolate."

Gradually Mai and Ryan started to venture back to activities together, starting with walking the dog and then extending to taking hikes and drives together. They began to socialize with friends, and when the kids came home for a week before their next school term started, the household almost felt normal again.

QUESTIONS FOR ASSESSING YOUR COMMUNICATION SKILLS

- Can you both admit when you are wrong?

- Do you both refrain from blame and criticism?

- Can you resolve conflicts peacefully?

- Is your partner flexible?

- Can you both emotionally regulate?

- Do you have a plan for conflict resolution?

- Do you use dialogue?

- Do you recognize each other's bids?

- Are you both getting better with attunement skills?

- Do you both use and recognize each other's need for a "time out"?

"Life doesn't make any sense without interdependence and the sooner we learn that we need each other the better for us all."
ERIK ERIKSON

CHAPTER TWELVE

MOVING FORWARD TOGETHER

"RELATIONSHIPS are always in motion," psychiatrists Richard Schwartz and Jacqueline Olds wrote in *Marriage in Motion*. When your attunement skills are good, you will recognize when there is too much distance in the relationship. If you have a concern, use the dialogue process to make sure you are reading the situation accurately. When you are comfortable with this format you can handle ruptures and repairs effectively, paying attention to how your partner is feeling, asking questions to clarify each other's needs, and showing willingness to negotiate, compromise, and be accountable.

When both of you reach the stage where mutual trust has begun to grow, the cycle of negative reactivity will no longer define your relationship. The process of building trust is the primary goal for the first year of relationship repair. It needs to occur on both sides of the partnership. The internal trust that the healing partner needs to build is not as obvious as what the wounded partner needs. The healing partner needs to develop trust that they can realize a positive result by practicing new behaviors. These new behaviors will become new habits and the default mode of relating.

This is the point where the partnership moves to the renewal stage: You have the skills to handle uncomfortable feelings in an effective way. You express concerns if you sense something is off. You both need to trust that being honest and accountable is the best choice, even if there is a period of upset. If you believe that raising an issue will result in more conflict or widen a rupture, you'll be heading back down the road to disconnection. When both partners are able to express a concern—confident that it will be heard and considered through mutual agreements about handling their differences—the trust is building to a place of renewed safety in their connection.

As long as each of you is willing to fully listen and validate your partner's concerns and to place a priority on keeping that emotional connection strong whenever it gets out of sync, you will be able to negotiate a path forward for each challenge.

As you move through these challenges and acquire new awareness and skills, you create a new feedback loop. You are creating more effective ways of dealing with anger, trust, and sexuality. Hopefully, you are now at that point in your relationship. Of course, you will experience a few hiccups along the way. Changing behaviors and patterns isn't easy, and it won't happen overnight. You can feel when your connection starts coming alive again when you start enjoying each other's company, actually laughing at each other's jokes, and having fun together.

In the next section, we address making the progress you have achieved a part of a new, more durable relationship for your future.

KEY POINTS

KEY POINTS FOR PART TWO

- Be accountable. Acknowledge and express remorse for deception and betrayal.
- Make a commitment to healing trust.
- Be honest and willing to come clean. Provide information and meet the hurt partner's conditions.
- Restructure boundaries with agreements.
- Provide transparency.
- Improve communication and conflict-repair and dialogue skills.
- Create a new connection with an emphasis on mutuality.

PART THREE
RENEWAL

*"Happiness is when what you think, what you say
and what you do are in harmony."*
MAHATMA GANDHI

*"The only person you are destined to become
is the person you decide to be."*
RALPH WALDO EMERSON

CHAPTER THIRTEEN

——

A NEW DYNAMIC

CONGRATULATIONS! You have courageously done a lot of work to get through the stages of repair. You both notice that your communication skills continue to improve. You give your partner the benefit of the doubt because you both have a commitment to transparency with your thoughts and feelings and a foundation of renewed trust. Your words and actions are consistent. You are flexible and open. And you let your partner know that they are appreciated and heard. You are able to listen and identify what is needed to keep attunement and connection strong on a daily basis. You realize that you learn from each other's different perspectives. You have let go of a need to be "right."

So, what happens now?

When you are having calm and effective discussions, it's a sign that you have created a new dynamic. You are now ready for the renewal stage of your relationship. This is the phase where the love you have for one another can begin to grow again, from the foundation of trust, honesty, and mutual understanding you have built.

This is not to say that everything will be rosy. There will be moments when the connection feels uncertain or you perceive a distance. Sometimes people cling to an idealized or romanticized view of what a relationship should be. They don't understand that all relationships take work at a certain point. There is a common misconception that a relationship won't work if there is any effort involved, especially in the early stages. On the contrary, a good connection takes effort and ongoing care over the long term. As important as nonverbal communication can be, couples need to remember the power of spoken appreciations and the need to negotiate expectations and not fall back on unspoken assumptions.

Harville Hendrix characterizes the space between two partners in a committed relationship as sacred, where you are mindful of what you are putting in that space. Your power is that you know how to ask questions, be attentive, and use good communication tools instead of letting the toxic elements of criticism, blame, and shaming enter that space. You will gain more confidence as you continue to use what you have learned and to experience the peace that comes with knowing the next right thing.

There are five essential skills that will help you keep a positive dynamic in your relationship: Mutuality, Attunement, Trust, Communication, and Honesty (MATCH).

Mutuality is a quality that keeps the emotional balance in place for a strong relationship. This is present when both partners feel that their needs and priorities are recognized by their mate.

Attunement means you empathize and understand one another—you are on the same wavelength.

Trust, as we have discussed, is the linchpin of any healthy relationship, which is, in turn, built upon a foundation of open **Communication** and **Honesty**. Without the foundation of trust, it is virtually impossible to build and sustain a strong relationship.

If you feel that your connection is slipping, pay attention to the mutuality, attunement, and communication in your dynamic. Do you have the interest and curiosity to understand what's important to your partner? How is the attunement in the relationship? Do you respond to each other's bids? Are you able to use effective techniques to resolve and repair differences? Do you have a solid foundation of trust with a commitment to honesty?

Keeping the acronym MATCH in mind is a good way to monitor your relationship skills.

THERAPY CREATES CHOICES

The ongoing work in therapy provides many benefits. Learning more about yourself and what you really value can help resolve internal conflicts. Through therapy you learn you can choose your responses and behaviors, that they are not automatic reactions to old ideas and beliefs that are outside your awareness.

Old wounds can still surface in the form of emotional triggers. But now you have perspective on these reactions and the skills to come to your own assistance. In addition to the new dynamic in your relationship, you will gain an increased awareness of how past experiences can trigger unwanted feelings and beliefs about yourself and others.

When you become conscious of that inner voice that speaks from an old and outworn narrative, you realize that you don't have to listen to it. That voice is operating from what are known as *internalized objects*. We all have inner voices that have internalized beliefs and expectations from our families and culture, perhaps a family expectation for everyone to conform or hold the same perspectives and views. These become our default beliefs and condition our responses. This lack of clear boundaries leads to what is known as enmeshment. It's a closed system that is highly resistant to outside influences. Through therapy you become aware of the limitations of that system and begin to see all of the other choices open to you.

When we have confidence that we don't need other's approval to validate ourselves, we can negotiate differences instead of creating a power struggle. We can respect our partner's perspective and acknowledge it. Sometimes we project notions upon our partner that have to do with our past wounds. Our bodies may tell us when a wound has been triggered in this regard. When you are receptive to other perspectives, you can identify ways that incorporate elements from both of your perceptions. But that won't happen if you are holding onto your views as though they are your life raft.

Kelly and Ugo (Part 3)

After attending extensive therapy separately as well as doing couples work with Kelly, Ugo came to understand more about the triggers he experienced whenever he felt

*Kelly was trying to control him. Specifically, Kelly's ac-
tions at times felt similar to the way Ugo's mother had
tried to control him. He recognized how reactively he be-
haved whenever he felt Kelly was being controlling. He
also noticed that he still carried anger from the powerlessness he felt as a child.*

*Ugo had a tendency to take an aggressive adolescent
stance of rebellion when he felt like he was being controlled. His feelings of powerlessness were too hard for
him to tolerate, and before he learned to identify them,
they would control him. The idea that he could shift his
perspective to come to his own assistance was foreign to
him. Ugo's therapy helped him see the choices he had as
an his adult, as opposed to that child who was dependent
on his parent for survival. He became aware of the difference between feelings and objective reality. He learned
how to accept the feelings as a valid reaction to his past
experiences but not to be controlled by them.*

*His strength and awareness increased as he learned
that feelings come and go. He was able to learn new ways
to cope when he was triggered by old feelings of powerlessness and resentment around control issues. When
Ugo was able to share this awareness with Kelly, she became much more conscious of how she communicated
with him. No longer were they caught in a destructive
cycle of mutual blame and recrimination.*

*This didn't mean that Kelly had to censor her com-
munication. She just learned to say things in a way that
didn't come across as critical and blaming. A small piece
of awareness had huge consequences for how they related
to each other.*

*Ugo and Kelly began Emotionally Focused Therapy
(EFT), a form of couples therapy that focuses on attachment and bonding in couples' relationships. It uses the
terms "raw spot" for when one of you is emotionally triggered by something your partner has done, for example,*

by a memory of betrayal or distrust. When one of you is experiencing a raw spot, this causes an attachment rupture, and you feel that you are not valued or your partner is not there for you. This wound can come from a thought about the betrayal, another hurtful past event, or because of feeling deprived, alone, or unappreciated. Kelly and Ugo learned how they each brought up these feelings in each other. Sue Johnson, the clinical psychologist who developed EFT, refers to this cycle as "the demon dialogue." When couples can see how the cycle has a life of its own and does not exist in their partner, they are changing this pattern.

Let's take a closer look at how Ugo and Kelly's communications style has changed.

COUPLES SESSION WITH UGO AND KELLY

Ugo: *I can see now how I was acting out. When you would ask me about other women I was spending time with, or questioning my work schedule —that was all perfectly reasonable. I was rebelling against things I thought of as intrusive. I would rebel by spending time with women I didn't even care about, almost as a way of saying to myself I can do what I want.*

Therapist: *Acting out this way would create reactions from Kelly that fit the narrative in your head. She would become upset and then start to act in a way that reinforced the story that you were making up.*

Ugo: *I can see that now. When I'm not giving Kelly reasons to distrust me, I don't overreact to normal questions. I'm not getting the criticism that I was expecting or waiting for.*

Kelly: *I felt like you would shut me out. And the more I felt shut out, the harder I would try to reach you. Then I would get angry and frustrated and start criticizing and* *blaming you. I guess my way of trying only made you want to retreat more.*

Ugo: *I didn't communicate. I was too filled with anger that I would keep directing at you. I didn't make the connection between the abuse from my childhood and the anger I felt.*

Therapist: *You both got caught in the demon dialogue. John Gottman says it's like the roach motel—you can check in, but you can't check out.*

Ugo: *I'm learning to choose my responses and get out of an automatic reaction.*

Therapist: *And when your son reached the age where you experienced the abuse, those feelings may have been triggered more and more.*

Ugo: *I just hope it's not too late. We've actually been having really good conversations, haven't we Kelly?*

Kelly: *It's like you've come back again after being gone for so many years.*

CONNECTION RITUALS

Establishing strong connection rituals will create more ease in the relationship. Even something as simple as a good morning kiss can set the pattern in motion and release oxytocin, the hormone for connection. Such rituals can help couples reconnect more easily when these opportunities are already in place. One person doesn't have to be the pursuer.

John Gottman has said that to keep a relationship strong there needs to be a 5:1 ratio of positive appreciations for every negative comment. I usually start or end every couples therapy session with "appreciations" between the couple. During the course of the repair, identifying positive qualities or actions regularly will help move the connection forward.

Ugo and Kelly started scheduling dinners together twice a week. Ugo had learned from the men in his group that he had to be the one to work at repairing the connection. He asked Kelly to do more activities together on the weekends. He suggested that they have a family game night on Sundays. Or they could go for a hike or go to the beach, or he could pitch balls to Paolo for him to practice his batting skills.

By establishing simple rituals, like weekly dinner or game nights, you can begin to regain a sense of connection that had been lost. These activities don't have to be elaborate. Allow yourself to be adventurous and find new ways of expressing joy and affection. A hug when you say hello or goodbye helps restore a level of intimacy. Schedule time to watch a favorite TV show, or watch the sunrise over cups of coffee. Constant novelty isn't necessary, but trying something new on a periodic basis can energize the relationship.

CONNECTING EXERCISES

1. Separately, make a list of 5 activities that each of you would like to do with your partner.

2. Find 2 activities that you will mutually enjoy or agree on and put them on your schedule.

3. Continue to do a weekly check-in to make time for a deeper look at feelings and concerns. You can vary the format to what is important for each of you with the 3-5 short check-in steps.

4. Use the 36 questions (included in the Appendix) as one of your connecting rituals. You can do one at a time, and you can take turns choosing a question. See the list of questions in the appendix.

ARTHUR ARON AND THE 36 QUESTIONS

A psychologist named Arthur Aron created a list of 36 questions for couples to ask each other. By responding to these questions, couples could develop a strong attraction. Aron actually said they would make people "fall in love with each other." Ask each other the questions to see the effect that they might have on your relationship as part of learning and curiosity about each other. If you want to read about one person's experience with the questions, read *How To Fall in Love with Anyone,* a memoir by Mandy Lin Catron.

GETTING OUTSIDE HELP

As we've noted, it is important while repairing a relationship to seek outside help, in the form of individual, couples, or group therapy, or a combination. We all have things that are outside of our awareness, and a therapist can help us consider different perspectives. Even after the repair process, however, you may find that scheduling a consultation with a couples therapist can help prevent eroding the progress you have made together. For example, if your physical connection is still unfulfilling, it's important to schedule a consultation with a therapist who specializes in human sexuality and who can help you understand how best to address your sexual intimacy issues.

Significant issues that are not addressed don't get healed, they fester. Over time they negatively impact the quality of trust.

Zoe and Jackson

Zoe tried to maintain hope that her relationship with Jackson would improve after he started therapy. She was taking care of herself and attending group and individual therapy sessions. But after she discovered web searches on his computer for S & M-type experiences, she began to wonder whom she had married. Zoe needed to understand who Jackson really was and, if he still loved her, how that love could be expressed.

As they both learned more about themselves through therapy, they began to understand how difficult childhood experiences had led them to cope in negative ways. Zoe's feelings of helplessness and abandonment had been exacerbated by Jackson's searches on Ashley Madison for hookups. His subsequent denial that he was actually looking for a sexual connection only made her feel more insecure. They hadn't been sexual for five years, and the betrayal made her question her own self-worth.

For his part, Jackson came to understand his maladaptive ways of reacting to feelings of obligation and being trapped. As Zoe demanded his attention, he withdrew into a world where he could be in control, searching for adventures that shut her out. Understanding what triggered these behaviors was just part of the repair. Now they had to find new ways to connect.

They were using the dialogue process, and there were no longer overt conflicts at home. But Zoe continued to feel a distance and a lack of emotional or physical intimacy. It seemed to her there was something missing in the transparency in their relationship and that there were parts of Jackson that seemed hidden. She felt that Jackson would make excuses for his lack of interest in sex. They were treating each other with consideration and scheduling things to do together, but the physical part of their relationship remained unsatisfying. Zoe tried to create opportunities and optimal settings to alleviate some of the concerns that Jackson had expressed. She booked an evening in a romantic couples' spa and an evening in a luxury hotel to no avail.

They had been working with a sex therapist, and during those sessions they both were able to talk about their concerns in a calm way. Jackson agreed to the exercises the therapist recommended. They also discussed ideas of things that they could do together during the week, like taking long walks or scheduling date nights. But they didn't prioritize those activities, so their couples' time happened sporadically. For example, they didn't go to bed at the same time, which took away from their opportunity to restore their intimate connection. After six months they had a break from couples therapy for the holidays, and neither of them felt motivated to continue.

Zoe told her support group that she was tired of being the pursuer. She said that when she backed off, Jackson didn't move forward. She was losing hope that they could ever have a satisfying sexual relationship or be on the same emotional wavelength. Even so, she resisted the idea of leaving Jackson. In her own therapy, Zoe was able to clarify her sense that Jackson wasn't able to make the kinds of changes she needed. She wanted a partner she felt connected to emotionally, sexually, and spiritually and no longer wanted to wait for Jackson to become the person she needed him to be.

The qualities that some people value at the start of a relationship may not be the ones that sustain the connection as time goes on. For Zoe, Jackson offered the pros-

pect of security. He was intelligent, ambitious, and his intense courtship flattered her. Jackson thought Zoe was beautiful and was in love with him. But their initial mutual attraction failed to grow into the kind of connection that can sustain and deepen a relationship over time.

Sometimes couples have different sexual needs that can't be bridged. One partner may have a particular sexual arousal template that doesn't work in the current relationship. It's very difficult for the couple when there can't be open communication about one's sexual preferences; these can become secrets that preclude transparency. If there are strong preferences that are part of one partner's sexual arousal template, and they can't be integrated into the couple's sexual style, then the potential for intimacy is limited. In that case, one or both parties may realize that this relationship needs to end in order for both partners to find sexual fulfillment. Letting yourself be known by your partner is necessary for deep intimacy. If there is a secret sexual arousal template, then that openness cannot be achieved.

FORGIVENESS

People often ask about forgiveness and how it figures into the process of repairing a relationship. I don't think forgiveness is entirely a decision, as some have said. I see forgiveness as a process that happens organically, in its own time, in its own way, without a specific timetable.

Over time the anger, hurt, resentment, and pain will dim and recede as your energy moves in new and expanded directions. When you live in an environment of respect and care and have a life that is fulfilling with good energy and loving people, the bad thoughts and feelings from the past will continue to be replaced with a satisfying present and future.

Parts of the process are unknowable. But it can be helped along with decisions you make about where to focus your mind, energy, and effort. Forgiveness happens when a space inside oneself that was once filled with painful feelings of sadness, resentment, and anger begins to focus on the kindness, support, caring, love, and understanding that you receive from self-care, your support circle, and your partner.

Forgiveness grows when the person who has caused the offense makes amends and honors you with respect, curiosity, and concern for your well-being. It continues to expand when a new and ongoing connection has a positive focus where you reinforce each other's learning.

Forgiveness happens alongside of healing and developing trust in yourself and your ability to choose people for your continuing story who will have your best interests at heart and who will work to support and understand you. It doesn't mean excusing behaviors or forgetting the past. It's that the experience that holds the pain becomes transformed and moves farther and farther into the past. Every day holds new possibilities—to learn, grow, and change—that are not dependent on anything but your own choices.

"A vision is not just a picture of what could be;
it is an appeal to our better selves,
a call to become something more."
ROSABETH MOSS KANTER

CHAPTER FOURTEEN

A NEW VISION

JUST AS AN ARCHITECT needs a vision that becomes a design, a blueprint, and eventually a building, a relationship requires a vision. That vision needs to be mutual, and both partners need to be aware of the steps and skills necessary to achieve it. Sometimes there was an unconscious or conscious vision at the start of the relationship that the couple outgrows or that changes for one or both of them. If the relationship is going to be renewed, there needs to be a vision for the present and future that is fulfilling for both partners.

Our universe is composed of systems—solar and biological systems, cultural and government systems, and social systems where the family is one of the most influential and integral in the early development of how we see the world. The family exists in partnership with other systems: friends, educational structures, and cultural influences. These influences all have a role in forming our complicated ideas about how things should be and how we should operate in relation to others and the world.

Each of you needs to commit to finding a nondestructive way of handling the inevitable differences and rough spots when they occur. Certain agreed-upon communication tools can keep disagreements from spiraling out of control. You never need to enter that danger zone where you are disrespecting each other. There's a big difference between bickering over small issues and unresolved conflict.

When Mai and Ryan constructed a vision statement for their future, they aligned on many issues. As they continued the deeper work in their couples therapy they were able to see how their families and their experiences growing up led to certain ideas they each held about how relationships should work. They also became aware of how needs that went unmet in their childhoods had created a longing for certain things that they had never spoken about. Ryan felt a strong obligation for financial success and to be a good provider. Mai felt a commitment to providing the family with structure and nurturing. They were able to see how they had each retreated to focusing on what they felt they had to do to keep the family going.

Ryan became aware that his family would never communicate directly about problems. Everyone would wait until the issues boiled over, to the point where anger and recrimination were the default emotions. The statement, "We communicate our concerns to each other without blame, criticism, or yelling," was an important addition for him and Mai to add to their relationship vision.

When you and your partner are reconstructing your relationship, there's an opportunity to discard some of the harmful or outworn beliefs, rules, and expectations. Now is the time to examine the qualities that you both want to see in the new relationship you are constructing. This task may sound daunting. I suggest starting very small, by noticing some things that might be topics to explore together and using the tools below to start the process.

Underlying the relationship there needs to be a shared set of values, for example, concerning family, finances, education, goals in life, parenting, and lifestyle. These, too, will affect the relationship going forward.

TOOLS

TOOLS FOR YOUR NEW RELATIONSHIP VISION

There are two exercises you can use to increase your clarity about what relationship fulfillment looks like for each of you: the Relationship Vision Drawing Exercise, and the Mutual Vision Exercise.

THE RELATIONSHIP VISION DRAWING EXERCISE

The Relationship Vision Drawing Exercise comes from a workshop with Patrick Carnes at the International Institute of Trauma and Addiction Professionals (IITAP) Institute; it works well for individuals and couples.

Each of you takes a blank sheet of 11x14-inch drawing paper. In the middle of the page, draw a circle large enough to accommodate five sentences. Then, around the circle, you each draw five pictures that represent your vision of where you and your partner will be in five years. The drawings can be very simple stick figures. By drawing your vision, you're using a different part of your brain than you would if you were to list these qualities in words. After you each have finished, share and explain your drawings to each other. Then work together on listing the steps you will need to take together to realize these dreams. Then you write the steps inside the circle. You may want to incorporate some of these mutual visions of your relationship into the lists that you each create in the next exercise.

When Kelly and Ugo did their vision drawing, they each drew a picture of a house with two adult figures and two children. They were able to translate these drawings into their goals of creating a family with two children and a house and list the steps of how they would reach that goal.

THE MUTUAL RELATIONSHIP VISION

The next exercise is from Imago Relationship Therapy (IRT), which emphasizes the importance of acknowledging differences and then negotiating for a win-win solution. Frequently we unintentionally bully or one-up each other with the idea that one of us is right and the other wrong. Imago Therapy emphasizes that by acknowledging their differences without feeling threatened, couples can create more acceptance and closeness. Bullying or pressuring your partner to see things your way, on the other hand, leads to alienation and conflict.

When couples incorporate the idea of differentiation, they are being clear about who they each are, clarifying boundaries and revealing themselves with honesty. Every relationship needs boundaries. Clarifying and respecting them is what allows us to be close and vulnerable. When the boundaries are clear, they actually allow for greater intimacy. Do you place a high priority on mutuality and emotional and physical connection? Then these need to be stated explicitly as priorities for this new vision of your relationship.

Start this exercise by each of you listing the qualities important in your ideal relationship. Then merge the two lists to create a blueprint for your relationship goals.

Here's an example of a Mutual Relationship Vision:

- We are truthful with each other.

- We have a fulfilling sex life.

- We use the dialogue process to get a difficult conversation back on track.

- We really listen and make sure we are understanding our partner's concerns.

- We express frustration at situations with moderation and not at our partner.

- We make requests instead of complaints.

- We check in with our partner's feelings about the relationship.

- We have the same values about sexual and emotional fidelity.

- We parent well together as a team.

- We each have private time for ourselves.

- We support our partner's interests.

- We value our sexual connection.

Jason and Mac (Part 3)

After Jason broke off the relationship with Mac, months passed. Summer was turning to fall, and as he crossed Washington Square Park and noticed the changing leaves, Jason realized it had been more than a year since he had last spoken to Mac. A few minutes later he saw a familiar figure moving toward him and found himself face-to-face with Mac, who asked, "How have you been, Jason?"

"Funny running into you here, Mac."

"Actually, I come this way now for my meeting," Mac said. After a few minutes of small talk, Mac moved to go, "Can't be late. Great seeing you, Jason."

A few days later Mac texted Jason that he had something he would really like to say in person. They agreed to meet in the park.

Jason was sitting on a bench as Mac walked up and handed him a thermos. "It's your favorite mix—kale, cucumber and kiwi," he said.

He went on, "Jason, I just want to tell you that it's taken me a year, but I think I'm starting to understand how badly I acted and how betrayed you felt. I'm really sorry and owe you a huge amends—more than just your favorite juice."

Jason saw that Mac's green eyes looked clearer than

he'd ever seen them.

"I went to Arizona for a while, and I learned a lot about myself. Since I came back to the city, I've been taking it one day at a time. I understand if you think we can't be friends."

After they parted, Jason hesitated for days before picking up the phone. He thought about all the stories he had heard in his group about how some partners learned from mistakes and others decided to go their separate ways. Eventually, though, he decided that he and Mac could meet again for a walk.

The next evening Jason told his group that Mac seemed different, quieter and he listened more. "His word and agreements are something that seem to mean something now, but I don't know if I can trust it."

"People change," one of the group suggested. "The hard part is that we can't predict when it will happen. All we can do is take care of ourselves and be cautious and mindful. If you think you want to give it another chance, you can take it slow and see what happens."

"Mac seems willing to provide any transparency I ask for," Jason said. "He is working the 12 steps. He wants to do a check-in, like a ritual, once a week, and he actually uses the dialogue! We are able to talk about things in a way we never could before."

Jason and Mac began to meet for weekly sessions with a therapist. Jason said he felt devalued and betrayed by Mac, whose deceptions and initial lack of remorse had thrown the relationship out of balance. Now Mac was willing to be vulnerable and make the emotional investments needed to reset the balance. They did a regular check-in to keep an ongoing dialogue about Mac's recovery, how they were each feeling, and what they needed and appreciated about each other. They agreed on a mutual vision for their relationship and the things that were important to each of them.

Mac and Jason learned to communicate with each other. Neither was trying to one-up the other. Mac learned to trust that when he used new behaviors, conflicts and differences could be resolved. They were able to communicate and form an agreement so problems didn't recur, and they expressed appreciation for this new dynamic and the skills they learned to keep it going. At their last session, Jason said he could see a value shift in Mac. "When Mac started saying the slogan from group—'My word is my bond' —I thought he was spouting a cliché. But now I think it's what he actually lives by."

THE KEYS TO A RENEWED RELATIONSHIP

- Pay attention to MATCH skills—Mutuality, Attunement, Trust, Communication, and Honesty

- Seek professional help with unresolved issues.

- Enhance sexual connection with intimacy skills.

- Craft a mutual relationship vision.

"The affirmation of one's own life, happiness, growth and freedom, is rooted in one's capacity to love."
ERICH FROMM

CHAPTER FIFTEEN

INTIMACY AND SEX

THE ROAD BACK to physical connection can be difficult even if both partners want to rekindle the flame. After a severe rupture and breach of trust, your sexual relationship won't pick up where it left off. But this can be an opportunity to create a new and mutually fulfilling intimate connection.

Physical intimacy can be one of the most powerful forces for strengthening your connection, but only if the intention is greater intimacy. As the esteemed sex therapist Barry McCarthy says, "The sexual paradox is that healthy sexuality has a positive 15 to 20 percent role in people's lives and relationship. However, dysfunctional, conflictual, or avoidant sexuality has a powerful destructive (50 to 75 percent) role in subverting the person and destabilizing the relationship."

You create erotic intimacy by using many of the skills we have explained in the repair process. Peggy Kleinplatz has studied optimal sexual experience over the past 15 years. Her research found that people reporting optimal sexual experiences emphasize openness, authenticity, empathy, and self-acceptance—the very qualities you have been working on. Couples who reported "magnificent" relationships also said that their focus became more pleasure oriented, and they each learned more about what they both wanted and how to create a quality of sex worth wanting. The couples Kleinplatz interviewed reported that great sex, not good sex, developed over time. The safety you have created for yourself and your partner is what will allow you to be flexible, let go, and be open to exploring new ways of relating physically.

Breaking down the barriers to intimacy requires being aware of how old ways of thinking can shape our responses and choices. You need to give yourself permission to explore new choices with your partner in order to create new outcomes. Expanding the frame of sex and intimacy means not letting moments of desire be the only motivator for erotic connection. There needs to be a willingness and intention to explore your own sources of pleasure. Opening up the sexual frame is about letting in new information and experiencing curiosity about how, when, and where you each experience pleasure. That includes all the sources of sensual and erotic pleasure, not just the experience of orgasm. In my research exploring women's motivation for sexual connection, the desire for intimate connection was far greater than the desire to experience orgasm. *All* of the models and motivations for sexual connection need to be included as the couple develops their own sexual style.

Connection and trust get progressively easier as a new dynamic becomes habitual. When transparency, accountability, agreements, and follow-through are present, along with emotional responsiveness and attunement, you will find it easier to be vulnerable with one another. Suzanne Iasenza, a New York City-based sex therapist with decades of experience treating couples with relationship, intimacy, and sexual issues, explains the importance of intentionality in creating a fulfilling erotic life. This means a willingness to push ahead, in spite of the risks, in order to create new outcomes.

We all have stories that we have constructed about ourselves and our experiences. Therapy helps us become more aware of how they were constructed, whether they are serving any useful purpose, and understanding that you have the power to reconstruct more adaptive stories. Iasenza's book *Transforming Sexual Narratives* explains the important role of challenging old beliefs that create barriers to intimacy by shaping our responses and choices. If you are hitting an impasse with physical connection, a sex therapist can help you identify how old beliefs and the trauma of betrayal may be prohibiting intimate connection.

In *Transforming Sexual Narratives*, Iasenza states, "The idea that someone doesn't deserve pleasure may not be a conscious thought, but could be an underlying unconscious narrative that a client may have been carrying around for a long time." If you are unaware of a prohibition, you can't challenge its validity. This process can start by simply identifying the thoughts and feelings that are present when you experience prohibitions in relation to sex. Many of the fears and anxieties, of course, will be related to the betrayal trauma. But by reducing all feelings to this incident you may be creating a narrative that consciously and unconsciously prohibits your body's natural response to a pleasurable sensation. As Iasenza states, "It's our bodies, not our heads that know how to receive pleasure, but we are rarely in our bodies."

There can be many sources for your thoughts and feelings, for example, judgments from the quality of the sexual life you had before. Now the objective is to observe these thoughts and feelings come and go without getting stuck in their content. Education about common assumptions and myths about sexuality can be helpful. Learning how to make more effective choices may rest on better information. In any case, it's time to let go of a sexual past that may have been unsatisfying.

Touch is an important expression of connection, and by adding this dimension to your connecting rituals you can experience another way of feeling cared for. Making touch part of your daily routine will create greater openness to communication.

Another tool for improving your intimate connection is sensate focus. This is a classic exercise developed by Masters and Johnson that has become a staple of sex therapy. It means creating an atmosphere of mindfulness by moving awareness away from disruptive thoughts that can shut down the body's receptivity to the pleasure of touch. It can take time and practice to keep bringing your focus back to your body's experience. The objective is to let the thoughts drift away and not to get stuck in conscious and unconscious judgments and prohibitions.

Setting aside a specific time and place for sensate focus gives both of you a clear way forward as well as a slow, safe, and intentional way to make progress. You make an agreement that you both show up at the appointed time and place. That takes away the pressure of one partner needing to initiate. Certain agreements, such as a limited time frame of 5-10 minutes in which either of you can signal if you would like to stop, with no judgment, can help reduce anxiety.

In *Erotic Intelligence* Alexandra Katehakis, the founder and clinical director of the Center for Healthy Sex, in Los Angeles, explains how intimacy involves the risk of letting yourself be fully known as you reveal your preferences and explore your sexuality with each other. She states, "Intimacy is finding new ways to know your partner, share struggles, ask for your needs to be met, be willing to change and keep dreams alive." The safety you have created for you and your partner is what will allow you to be flexible, let go, and be open to exploring new ways of relating physically.

In the case of Mai and Ryan, their attempts at renewing their physical relationship were similar to what many couples experience. They planned a weekend getaway. Mai said she wanted to reconnect sexually, but after she returned, she expressed disappointment at that part of the weekend. "We went hiking in the Catskills and had a great time. The only disappointment is that we are having a hard time reconnecting physically. We had the intention to do sensate, but it just didn't happen."

This often occurs when couples are learning to connect again. It takes time for each partner to feel safe.

STEPS TO IMPROVE YOUR PHYSICAL CONNECTION

#1 EXPAND YOUR NOTION OF WHAT "SEX" IS

You want to broaden your idea of sex beyond intercourse to make room for all the ways you can experience erotic pleasure. Take the focus off the goal of reaching orgasm; allow yourself to go slow and relax with all of the many ways you can experience sensuality and erotic pleasure. The pleasure might come from a warm feeling of closeness. Learning all of the things that make your partner feel in touch with their sensuality will heighten the arousal process as it builds from experiencing your partner's responses.

#2 MAKE TIME TO NURTURE PHYSICAL CONNECTION

This process won't start until you both agree on a time and place to start connecting. I used to see couples who would sit around waiting for each other to initiate this. Some couples complain that it doesn't feel "natural" to plan this time. But if you think back to when you first met, there was planning involved in connecting, you didn't always run into each other.

Allow the naturalness to come back gradually. Get comfortable with stopping at any point, letting your partner know in a gentle way that it's okay to turn down an invitation to connect physically. These are important things to discuss so you both will be comfortable with these choices.

The connection might feel awkward and uncomfortable if there has been a long break. Reassure yourself that this is normal and natural. Accept these feelings as part of the process of creating something new and better. Don't impose old narratives and beliefs on these feelings.

If your relationship is blocked in this area, it's important to acknowledge this. You can't fix something that you can't acknowledge. This is where the dialogue process can help with a gentle but direct way of making a request. It's important not to blindside your partner with a discussion about intimacy. Remember the dialogue process emphasizes requesting a mutually agreeable time to express a concern. If you don't honor this step, you can be sabotaging the discussion from the outset. When your partner agrees to a time to hear your concern, you can say that your physical connection seems to be stuck and you would like to make a plan for working on this part of your relationship. In the dialogue, your partner will then mirror what you are saying. This creates the connection that's needed to move to the step of problem solving.

#3 ENLIST ALL OF YOUR SENSES

Create an environment that helps to enhance your experience of pleasure. Take the time to nurture this connection and expand the possibilities into many realms of sensuality. Music, scented candles, food, and drink can be employed to enhance your senses. The skin is the largest sensory area, and you can enhance the pleasure of touch by using a soft feather duster or lotions. You can use the focus on the sensation of touch to take small, safe steps.

Iasenza suggests that couples each list ways they experienced pleasure through their five senses during one day. This could include feeling your body's movement on a run or the pleasure of swimming in cool water on a hot day. It could be the smell and taste of a favorite food, hearing the sounds of nature, or seeing the changing colors in the evening sky. The point is to increase your awareness of the experiences of pleasure—to bring them into your consciousness and connect them with your ability to make choices.

Create an environment that helps to enhance your experience of pleasure. Take the time to nurture this connection and expand the possibilities into many realms of sensuality.

#4 PRACTICE EROTIC TOUCH

When I first started giving these instructions to couples, some reported giving each other sports type massages. There's nothing wrong with an energetic massage, but this is not what we are talking about. We're trying to work with a softer, more erotically focused form of touch, one not specifically goal-directed toward arousal. When you first start, limit the touch to 5 minutes with each partner in the roles of giver and receiver. When you are in the receiver position, you can close your eyes and focus on the sensation of how touch can feel pleasurable. You both work on learning how to create this pleasure for each other and let yourselves relax enough to allow your body to tune in to its own sensations without being blocked by messages from your mind.

#5 SLOW DOWN AND LET YOUR MIND AND BODY WORK TOGETHER

You are connecting your mind and body and letting them get in sync. Learn to manage this experience internally without your mind's interfering and shutting down your body's responses. When someone has used sex as a way to numb and distract from painful feelings, they count on sex for feelings of intensity to distract them from self-doubts and other difficult feelings. What we are doing here is learning to accept the feelings that will come up, as we start to connect in a new way.

Slow down and allow yourself to experience pleasure, arousal, and erotic feelings as they come, with no pressure to make them happen. The presence of an erection doesn't mean this is the time to move forward. Mutuality is about being in sync with your partner and developing signals and ways of communicating to move forward together in a pleasurable erotic space. Allow yourselves the time and stimulation to reach an optimal state. This is what Dr. Kleinplatz referred to when she identified communication as one of the key elements for optimal sex. Allow erections to come and go and stay in touch with the rhythm of each other's response with good attunement.

As Harville Hendrix has said, "Clear communication is a window into the world of your partner; truly being heard is a powerful aphrodisiac."

#6 BECOME A "BLACK-BELT COMMUNICATOR"

Kleinplatz's study of optimal sex makes the point that magnificent sex isn't about techniques or novelty. She actually identified communication as one of the most important characteristics. She says people who report optimal sexual experiences are black-belt communicators. Continue to improve the ways you and your partner communicate gently and effectively on sensitive issues.

#7 MINDFULNESS PRACTICE

Use mindfulness practice to help with intrusive thoughts that will shut down your body's ability to recognize pleasure. With mindfulness, you focus completely on the sensation of the moment. You detach from a narrative in your head that, especially for women, often shuts down your body's ability to respond. Use some of the techniques for alleviating distress to soothe your mind. Focus on your breath coming in and out. Visualize your safe place or another calming or erotic scene. When you shift into this mode, you are shutting down your disturbing narrative. These experiences are designed as short sensory holidays from your mind's never-ending stream of commentary.

Let go of any distractions that are shutting down your body's ability to respond. Don't be drawn into an internal power struggle with your unconscious. Gently notice your thoughts and feelings. If you are comfortable doing so, share your thoughts or fears with your partner; this gives them the chance to provide reassurance. If you're not comfortable with sharing, write the thoughts and feelings in your journal. Or you can just let them float away.

You need to learn to let go of many of the barriers that the mind uses to shut down the body's response. These beliefs can thwart the body's response to arousal in either gender. We want to capture the beliefs that still hold us captive and release them, for example, the idea that we can't experience eroticism unless we are already aroused. This puts undue pressure on a connecting experience and isn't the way the human sexual response cycle works. Men's sexual response cycle is often more straightforward than women's; they move from excitement to orgasm to resolution. But women's response cycle is more variable. After a certain age many women complain of feeling out of touch with their eroticism. Emily Nagoski's book *Come as You Are* and her TED talk are excellent resources for understanding more about how our mind and body work together in these areas.

As in the exercises for calming the mind, you don't want to oppose disturbing thoughts; that increases their energy. Just gently notice them as if you were out of your body, watching them float by.

#8 EXCHANGE SENSUAL MENUS

Write down three things that enhance your sensual feelings. Iasenza has each partner create menus of pleasure for themselves. This isn't confined to erotic pleasure. Iasenza uses this exercise to increase awareness of the potential to receive pleasure through all of your senses. Sharing these sensual menus with each other will deepen your connection.

Some couples enjoy reading to each other in bed, getting

a foot massage, or a certain specific sexual act. What kind of foreplay makes you feel closer to your partner and more relaxed? Continue these exchanges as part of the process of building more enjoyable sensual experiences as you become more attuned to what you like and allowing your partner to have a window into different parts of your experience. Intimacy grows with overcoming the fears of letting yourself be known, as you create more mutuality and shared vulnerability in all aspects of your lives.

#9 SHARE SENSUAL ENHANCERS

This is where you work by yourself and with your partner to find what enhances your erotic feelings. Share a scene from a movie or a passage from a book. Suggest trying certain sensual prompts with your eyes closed, things your partner might enjoy. Try different tastes, smells, textures. You might enjoy certain kinds of music or sounds, like waves crashing or a rain shower. You can incorporate these experiences into the touching exercises. The value is in the *process* of sharing and the openness to receiving and participating together in these experiences.

#10 TAKE RISKS IN LETTING YOURSELF BE KNOWN

As you continue to share your sensual menus with each other, you can let more of yourself be known to your partner. You're building on the qualities for optimal sex with openness, authenticity, empathy and self-acceptance.

"You never change things by fighting the existing reality.
To change something, build a new model
that makes the existing model obsolete."
R. BUCKMINSTER FULLER

CHAPTER SIXTEEN

FLOW

T IS BEING in the state of flow that makes experience genuinely satisfying, says Mihaly Csikszentmihalyi, in his classic book, *Flow: The Psychology of Optimal Experience.* What is flow? Csikszentmihalyi describes it as the state where our thoughts and feelings—our consciousness—are integrated in pleasurable and totally absorbing moments. Sometimes it's called "being in the zone," the feeling and focus of a tennis player watching the ball coming across the court or in receiving a lover's kiss or looking at the smile on your baby's face.

DURING A FLOW STATE

- Your mind or consciousness is free of distractions
- You are balanced between challenge and ability
- You relax by being absorbed in the moment
- You are effortlessly absorbed without strain or worry

THE TRUST SOLUTION

- Your perception of time is altered

- Your actions and consciousness melt together, and you feel at one with activity

Achieving flow, which is the goal as you renew your relationship, is a day-to-day, conscious, ongoing process of building and reinforcing new behaviors, insights, skills, and habits. Building connection and trust gets progressively easier as a new dynamic becomes habitual. If you are following the repair steps, trust will have started to grow again like a sapling seeking sunlight. To survive, it needs protection, nurturing, and attention.

We have the ability to control where we focus our energy and attention. Something doesn't become interesting until it has our attention. When you focus your attention on the connection with your partner, you develop the interest—the curiosity—that's necessary to renew your relationship. As Thich Nhat Hanh states, the gift we give our partner is that of truly paying attention. Many couples come to therapy feeling hurt and rejected because of a lack of interest from their partner.

To experience flow in a relationship, you have to invest psychic energy. When we make a conscious decision to focus and share our dreams, interests, ideas, emotions, and activities with our partners we create the opportunity for our interest in them to grow and the connection to take on the characteristics of flow.

Ryan and Mai, Ugo and Kelly, Jason and Mac, Blair and Marcus, and Carrie and Mick all worked hard at the process of repair with its ups and downs and continuing challenges. They all had the willingness and determination to focus their attention on what was needed for repair. They didn't get derailed by beliefs about what *should* happen. They learned that in life and relationships there is constant change along with things that remain steady. They understood the need for flexibility. You need to revisit your assumptions and expectations as you learn more about yourself and your partner.

Achieving intimacy requires the desire to know the other person and have interest and curiosity about their inner life. Mutuality and attunement require attention to how your partner is feeling, questioning to clarify their needs, and a willingness to negotiate, compromise, and be accountable. It means extending yourself beyond your comfort zone and accepting the stance of not knowing. If you don't have interest in what your partner is thinking and feeling, about their needs and satisfactions, their goals, dreams, and fulfillment, it will be hard to pay attention. It's hard to fake it—and you shouldn't try.

When transparency, accountability, agreements, and follow-through are present, along with mutuality and attunement, the process of renewal takes on a life of its own. The psychoanalyst Erich Fromm reminds us of the limits in Western culture's sometimes prevalent idea that love should be a spontaneous emotional reaction. "An important factor in erotic love is that of *will*," he wrote in *The Art of Loving*. "To love somebody is not just a strong feeling —it is a decision, it is a judgment, it is a promise."

In my experience, the couples who succeed have one thing in common: They all decided to make the repair of their relationship a priority. It became an unshakeable commitment and the primary focus of their attention. They learned the skill of being a two-person system. They clarified where their

vision of fulfillment and happiness was united. They were realistic about inevitable differences and acquired the tools to
handle them effectively. They had the openness and curiosity
that expanded their perspective and allowed them to search
for new and creative ways to operate with mutuality and attunement. They showed a commitment to staying open to
learning what was needed, in spite of uncomfortable feelings
and difficult moments. They saw that by healing their relationships, they could also change old, unconscious patterns
and beliefs that limited how they approached life's inevitable
challenges. They learned that their relationship could be a
crucible in which they became their best selves. They said
that their connection and intimacy got better through the
years. They all agreed that the fulfillment in their relationship
grew and became stronger from all they had gone through.

Happiness, growth, self-awareness, freedom, and
self-acceptance are all part of the rewards we will experience as our faith in what we are capable of becoming continues to build. I hope that over the years you will continue
to grow in intimacy, attunement, and fulfillment where the
pleasure of your connection results in a positive state of
flow, where daily life together—making decisions and sharing reactions and experiences—will become the greatest
pleasure in your life.

KEY POINTS

KEY POINTS FOR PART THREE

- A new relationship dynamic is formed by consistency in words and actions, transparency, and good communication and listening skills.

- Both partners understand and accept that all relationships take work at various points in time.

- Practicing MATCH skills—mutuality, attunement, trust, communication, and honesty—protects the health and well-being of the relationship.

- Seeking professional help when needed for tune-ups or when there is a rough patch that goes unresolved is a wise choice.

- Establishing and using regular connecting rituals keeps intimacy alive.

- Both partners work together to craft a new, mutual vision of their priorities and values.

- Attention to sexuality enhances connection and intimacy.

- The strong connection from this renewal results in a state of flow for a fulfilling relationship.

— APPENDIX —

TOOLS FOR THE REPAIR PROCESS

EMOTIONAL REGULATION SKILLS

Immediately after discovery of a betrayal, there will be a need to cope with intense emotions and distress. Examples of tools to calm the emotional storm are affirmations, visualization, imagining a safe place, breathing, mindfulness practice, naming feelings, recognizing cognitive distortions, keeping a gratitude journal, and "move a muscle—change a thought."

ACCOUNTABILITY STATEMENT
AMENDS LETTER

During the period after the betrayal is discovered, the hurt partner will feel an intense need for information about what actually happened, as opposed to the version of reality that the betraying partner tried to present. In an accountability statement or amends letter the healing partner states their accountability for the impact of their behaviors on the relationship. The statement can start the repair process before a formal disclosure takes place. It's a tool that puts the healing partner's intentions into words as part of their initial step of being accountable.

BOUNDARY SETTING

It's important to set clear boundaries and agreements and to stick to them. The inclusion of a time element is important. An example is, "I will inform you within 24 hours if I have not observed a boundary," or "I will let you know within 24 hours if the person I was seeing outside our relationship tries to contact me." Such clear, time-bound agreements provide safety for the hurt partner, who fears discovering another lie or betrayal. They need to feel a degree of certainty that their partner will not lie or deceive them if they are going to have a future together. The healing partner's ability to be honest will be crucial in rebuilding trust.

FORMAL DISCLOSURE

A disclosure is the start of a process to provide the transparency that repairing trust requires. A formal disclosure process is the most effective way to deal with the hurt partner's need for information. This should be done if the hurt partner would like to have this information and when and if they are comfortable doing the disclosure.

A disclosure process is a meeting between the healing and the hurt partners where the healing partner admits to incidents of sexual betrayal and answers questions that the hurt partner has prepared. The healing partner needs to answer their mate's questions and to inform them about their actions, including when, where, and with whom the betrayal happened. The healing partner needs to disclose their attempts to obscure their behaviors by identifying instances of deceit and gaslighting.

This meeting is usually facilitated by a therapist who specializes in intimate betrayal and relationship recovery. In-depth preparation is necessary to ensure the best outcome, and both the hurt partner's and the healing partner's therapists are present to provide support.

Once the hurt partner requests a disclosure and the healing partner agrees, it is important to take the following steps:

1. Make an agreement for a formal disclosure process, setting a date, and working with therapists who can support both of you.

Usually, it's best to set a date one month to six weeks after the discovery or admission of the rupture. The hurt partner needs plenty of time to establish a support system and develop and practice emotional regulation and distress-tolerance skills as part of their preparation.

2. Work with an experienced therapist to prepare for the disclosure.

Professional guidance is imperative to support the process of revealing hurtful information that was part of the intimate betrayal. Preparation and support are critical to a disclosure's success. Initial information that may have been revealed when the betrayal was discovered does not eliminate the need for this process. The hurt partner needs to know the truth to heal. A formal disclosure prevents the retraumatizing that occurs when there is staggered disclosure with more hurtful information coming out in dribs and drabs.

3. The hurt partner prepares a list of the questions that they want answered.

4. The healing partner prepares information for disclosure.

If the partner is in recovery for sex addiction or problematic sexual behavior, this would include all of the ways that they acted out. It includes the time periods involved, how they tried to hide or lied about the actions, and information about money spent and other ways their behavior impacted their partner. The Recommended Reading section has a list of books about the disclosure process.

IMPACT AND RESTITUTION LETTERS

Stefanie Carnes' healing model for partners, outlined in her book *Courageous Love: A Couples Guide to Conquering Betrayal*, includes what she terms Impact and Restitution Letters. In her model, these are written by each of the partners after a formal disclosure where all of the offending behaviors have been revealed.

Impact Letter

An impact letter is a tool that supports healing. It gives the hurt partner the opportunity to express the painful ramifications of the betrayal in a well-thought-out manner. The impact letter is often shared in a couples therapy session after a formal disclosure. In her book Carnes includes worksheets to help in the letter's preparation as well as an example of an impact letter.

Restitution Letter

Carnes suggests writing a restitution letter after a formal disclosure. Written by the healing partner to the hurt partner, the restitution letter expresses their remorse and responsibility for the pain caused by their actions and their intentions for the future.

CREATE AGREEMENTS

Agreements need to be detailed and specific. One of the traps many couples fall into is that the agreements they make are too vague They should be measurable, time-limited, and have accountability. Example: "I will tell you within 24 hours if my affair partner tries to contact me or if I try to contact her. And I will not respond until we have discussed this."

Don't break agreements without negotiation.

For example, this would include an agreement about the specific time and frequency when the couple will do a check-in.

Put major agreements in writing.

This is what provides accountability and is often a good idea for key provisions, such as contact with the affair partner or other critical factors that may make or break deals in the relationship. Agreements should describe how transparency will be provided: What is the agreement about boundaries and contacts with certain people, places, and things? Will the hurt partner have passwords and access to the healing partner's computer, email, phone, and social media accounts?

Here is an example of a written agreement:

DATE

_____

AGREEMENT BETWEEN

_____

Elements of agreement: I will not meet with Robert outside of work gatherings and will talk with him only with other people present. I will tell him that I'm not comfortable texting and emailing about personal issues. If he makes an attempt to contact or meet with me, I will let you know within 24 hours.

Signed by both partners:

_____

_____

THREE CIRCLES TOOL

The three circles tool simplifies and defines how behaviors need to be changed. This tool can be used for any relationship where accountability and honesty have been compromised.

This is an example of a possible three circles diagram.

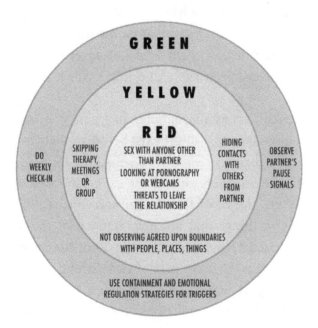

The inner, red circle includes behaviors that you both agree are totally off-limits. These can be things such as having sex with anyone other than each other, looking at pornography, or having contact with any acting-out partners.

The middle or yellow circle contains behaviors that lead to the red circle and need to be avoided. These include guidelines for how you put yourself in danger with people, places, and things with specific agreements about them. The yellow circle could include spending time alone with women friends the partner is not comfortable with. If pornography use was a problem, it could be spending time alone on the computer.

The outer or green circle includes positive behaviors that you want to increase. These are actions that nurture the connection, support recovery, and move relationship-repair forward. Examples of these would be attending therapy meetings, checking in with a sponsor (someone with substantial recovery time of their own who has agreed to guide you in your recovery process), and doing a check-in with your partner.

The circles act as a visual plan of where you want to establish boundaries that didn't exist before or that were transgressed. The three circles aren't a substitute for sound judgment. They exist to create realistic expectations and clarity, and they are the basis for certain agreements. Of course, there will be things that are not included in the diagram. The three circles lay out clear examples of the most crucial behavior changes that are part of establishing transparency, accountability, and trust. They can define specific behaviors that you both agree are violations of trust. Even so, gray areas and subtle distinctions will arise. If there is a rupture around these issues, the couple needs to be able to discuss these distinctions without anger.

THE CHECK-IN

The check-in is one of the tools that most partners request to support their healing process. The check-in provides transparency and accountability and establishes a better connection and new communication patterns. As with all of the tools, the check-in is best when it is initiated by the healing partner. This goes a long way to building trust and showing commitment to repair.

1. Make an agreement for a regular time to do the check-in. The healing partner must initiate the process. The hurt partner will know things are off track if they have to remind the healing partner or chase after them for the check-in. Some couples do the check-in daily at first and then move to once a week, according to what the hurt partner would like.

2. Agree on the components of the check-in. You both can agree on what can be accomplished, such as identifying feelings, sobriety time accomplished, needs or concerns, positive or challenging situations you each experienced, and what you each appreciated about the other. It's best to keep the list short and keep the exchange to 15-30 minutes. It can be adjusted from time to time as needs change.

3. It's important that the check-in become a ritual in your relationship with a regular day and time. Keep it short, such as 15 minutes, so it is easy to schedule. This tool goes a long way toward rebuilding trust and answers many elements of the repair process—transparency, accountability, agreements, follow-through, empathy, and communication.

4. When I see a deterioration in the couple's connection during the trust-building process, it al-

most always happens when the check-in has been neglected. It is certainly an option for the couple to agree to modify the check-in after a period of stability, but it is important that this be a mutual and not a unilateral decision.

5. One example of a check-in model is FANOS, designed by Debra and Mark Laaser and described in Debra's book, *Shattered Vows*. FANOS is an acronym for feelings, affirmation, needs, own, and sobriety.

Here is one formula for this process:

- Put words on some current **Feelings**

- State an **Affirmation** or appreciation (clarify)

- Identify **Needs** —something you need but not necessarily from your partner

- **Own**—take responsibility or apologize for something you said or did

- **Sobriety**—the status of your sobriety/the number of days since acting out

THE DIALOGUE PROCESS

The dialogue process is one of Imago Therapy's central tools. It has been modified by many practitioners and has become a common formula for effective communication. It's sometimes called reflective listening.

Harville Hendrix, the originator, teaches a specific format that I find effective. The dialogue eliminates a power struggle or one person's trying to hijack the conversation back to their concerns. The structure of taking turns prevents the breakdown of communication and the escalation of anger and frustration. The process needs to be practiced and used to understand how effective it is.

Here's a summary of the steps:

DIALOGUE STEPS FOR SENDER

1. Ask your partner for time to express your concern. (They should give you a time that works for them.)

2. Express your concern briefly with no blame or criticism.

3. After they mirror it, let them know if they got it.

DIALOGUE STEPS FOR RECEIVER

1. Mirror. Summarize your partner's concern. Ask if you "got it." If they say, "no," ask them to repeat and try again to mirror.

2. Validate. Tell them *what* makes sense about this concern. This does not mean you agree. It means that you can understand their feelings from their perspective. (This demonstration of empathy will go a long way to smoothing disagreements, healing ruptures, and strengthening your relationship.)

3. Optional Step. After you validate and ask if you got it, you can ask them what they think will help

with the resolution of the concern. Ask for one way that you might meet an immediate need that is causing distress. What action could have a positive effect?

36 QUESTIONS

These 36 questions were developed by psychologist Arthur Aron as an experiment to determine if by asking each other these increasingly probing questions, two people would develop increased feelings of intimacy and closeness. Try asking them with your partner, and see what happens.

Find a time when you and your partner have at least 45 minutes free and are able to meet in person.

For 15 minutes, take turns asking one another the questions in Set I below. Each person should answer each question, but in an alternating order, so that a different person goes first each time.

After 15 minutes, move on to Set II, even if you haven't yet finished the Set I questions. Then spend 15 minutes on Set II, following the same system.

After 15 minutes on Set II, spend 15 minutes on Set III.

Note: Each set of questions is designed to be more probing than the previous one. The 15-minute periods ensure that you spend an equivalent amount of time at each level of self-disclosure.

SET I
1. Given the choice of anyone in the world, whom would you want as a dinner guest?

2. Would you like to be famous? In what way?

3. Before making a telephone call, do you ever rehearse what you are going to say? Why?

4. What would constitute a "perfect" day for you?

5. When did you last sing to yourself? To someone else?

6. If you were able to live to the age of 90 and retain either the mind or body of a 30-year-old for the last 60 years of your life, which would you want?

7. Do you have a secret hunch about how you will die?

8. Name three things you and your partner appear to have in common.

9. For what in your life do you feel most grateful?

10. If you could change anything about the way you were raised, what would it be?

11. Take four minutes and tell your partner your life story in as much detail as possible.

12. If you could wake up tomorrow having gained any one quality or ability, what would it be?

SET II

13. If a crystal ball could tell you the truth about yourself, your life, the future, or anything else, what would you want to know?

14. Is there something that you've dreamed of doing for a long time? Why haven't you done it?

15. What is the greatest accomplishment of your life?

16. What do you value most in a friendship?

17. What is your most treasured memory?

18. What is your most terrible memory?

19. If you knew that in one year you would die suddenly, would you change anything about the way you are

now living? Why?

20. What does friendship mean to you?

21. What roles do love and affection play in your life?

22. Alternate sharing something you consider a positive characteristic of your partner. Share a total of five items.

23. How close and warm is your family? Do you feel your childhood was happier than most other people's?

24. How do you feel about your relationship with your mother?

SET III

25. Make three true "we" statements each. For instance, "We are both in this room feeling..."

26. Complete this sentence: "I wish I had someone with whom I could share..."

27. If you were going to become a close friend with your partner, please share what would be important for them to know.

28. Tell your partner what you like about them; be very honest this time, saying things that you might not say to someone you've just met.

29. Share with your partner an embarrassing moment in your life.

30. When did you last cry in front of another person? By yourself?

31. Tell your partner something that you like about them [already].

32. What, if anything, is too serious to be joked about?

33. If you were to die this evening with no opportunity to communicate with anyone, what would you most regret not having told someone? Why haven't you told them yet?

34. Your house, containing everything you own, catches fire. After saving your loved ones and pets, you have time to safely make a final dash to save any one item. What would it be? Why?

35. Of all the people in your family, whose death would you find most disturbing? Why?

36. Share a personal problem and ask your partner's advice on how they might handle it. Also, ask your partner to reflect back to you how you seem to be feeling about the problem you have chosen.

DOS AND DON'TS
FOR EACH PARTNER

For the hurt partner:

- Do honor your intuitive senses

- Commit to focusing on good self-care

- Discuss your concerns as they arise with a support group

- Forgive yourself for not recognizing the problem sooner

- Make sure you have a reliable support system in place

- Be very careful about whom you confide in

- Make your partner's getting treatment a condition for continuing the repair process

- Learn to identify needed boundaries and implement them

- Learn to name the emotions as they fluctuate inside you

- Learn self-soothing techniques and use them for emotional regulation

- Learn to identify options instead of staying focused on your first default reaction

- Practice gentle observer stance

- Don't make permanent long-term decisions for the first six months

- Don't have unprotected sex for the first year
- Get tested for STDs and other infections
- Get legal and financial advice early on
- Protect yourself financially
- Educate yourself about addictions, sex addiction, sexuality, betrayal, and trauma

For the healing partner:
- Be impeccable with your word
- Listen without judging or defending
- Don't use sex for power and control
- Spend regular time with your partner
- Practice a period of sexual abstinence
- Admit mistakes freely
- Practice humility and openness to new learning
- Seek out responses on your behaviors from people in your support group and from your therapist
- Recognize your defensiveness and denial
- Encourage members of your support group to call you on your problematic behaviors
- Be consistent in your attendance at therapy and support group
- Identify online groups to supplement in person groups
- Find a therapist with appropriate credentials

RECOMMENDED READING

BETRAYAL

C. Black, *Intimate Treason: Healing the Trauma for Partners Confronting Sex Addiction* (Las Vegas, NV: Central Recovery Press, 2012).

S. Carnes, ed. *Mending a Shattered Heart: A Guide for Partners of Sex Addicts* (Carefree, AZ: Gentle Path Press, 2nd ed., 2011).

S. Carnes, *Facing Heartbreak: Steps to Recovery for Partners of Sex Addicts* (Carefree, AZ: Gentle Path Press, 2012).

J. Freyd and P. Birrel, *Blind to Betrayal: Why We Fool Ourselves We Aren't Being Fooled* (NY: John Wiley and Sons, 2003).

S. Glass, *Not Just Friends: Rebuilding Trust & Recovering Your Sanity After Infidelity* (NY: Free Press, 2004).

C. Jorgensen Sheets, *Helping Her Heal: An Empathy Workbook for Sex Addicts to Help Their Partners Heal* (Long Beach, CA: Sano Press, 2019).

D. Laase, *Shattered Vows: Hope and Healing for Women Who Have Been Sexually Betrayed* (Grand Rapids, MI: Zondervan, 2008).

M. Mays, *The Aftermath of Betrayal* (Leesburg, VA: Relational Recovery Press, 2017).

V. Tidwell Palmer, *Moving Beyond Betrayal: The 5-Step Boundary Solution for Partners of Sex Addicts* (Las Vegas, NV: Central Recovery Press, 2016).

M. Scheinkman, "Beyond the Trauma of Betrayal: Reconsidering Affairs in Couple Therapy," *Family Process*, 44(2), 227-244.

J. Schneider and M. Corley, *Surviving Disclosure: A*

Painter's Guide for Healing the Betrayal of Intimate Trust (Charleston, SC: Recovery Resource Press, 2012).

J. Schneider, *Back From Betrayal: Recovering from His Affairs* (Charleston, S.C.: Recovery Resources Press, 2015).

J. Abrams Spring, *After the Affair: Healing the Pain and Rebuilding the Trust When a Partner Has Been Unfaithful* (NY: Harper, 3rd ed., 2020).

B. Steffens, *Your Sexually Addicted Spouse: How Partners Can Cope and Heal* (Far Hills, NY: New Horizon Press, 2009).

R. Weiss, *Out of the Doghouse: A Step By Step Relationship-Saving Guide for Men Caught Cheating* (Deerfield Beach, FL: Health Communications Inc., 2017).

ADDICTION

P. Carnes, *Don't Call it Love* (NY: Bantam, 1991).

P. Carnes, *Facing the Shadow* (Carefree, AZ: Gentle Path Press, 2005).

P. Carnes, *The Betrayal Bond* (Deerfield Beach, FL: Health Communications Inc., 1997).

L. Hatch, *Relationships in Recovery: A Guide for Sex Addicts Who Are Starting Over* (Santa Barbara, CA: Pentacle, 2013).

A. Katehakis, *Sex Addiction as Affect Dysregulation: A Neurobiologically Informed Holistic Treatment* (NY: W. W. Norton, 2016).

K. McDaniel, *Ready to Heal: Women Facing Love, Sex and Relationship Addiction* (Carefree, AZ: Gentle Path Press, 2012).

R. Weiss, *Sex Addiction 101: A Basic Guide to Healing from Sex, Porn and Love Addiction* (Deerfield Beach, FL: Health Communications Inc., 2015).

COUPLES

S. Carnes, *Courageous Couples: A Couples Guide to Conquering Betrayal* (Carefree, AZ: Gentle Path Press, 2020).

J. Gottman, *The Science of Trust: Emotional Attunement for Couples* (NY: W. W. Norton, 2011).

J. Gottman and N. Silver, *The Seven Principles for Making Marriage Work* (NY: Harmony Books, 2015).

H. Hendrix and H. LaKelly Hunt, *Making Marriage Simple: Ten Truths for Changing the Relationship You Have into the One You Want* (NY: Harmony Books, 2013).

H. Hendrix, *Getting the Love You Want* (NY: St. Martin's Griffin, reprint, revised, updated ed., 2019).

S.M. Johnson, *Hold Me Tight: Seven Conversations for a Lifetime of Love* (NY: Little, Brown, 2008).

S.M. Johnson, *The Practice of Emotionally Focused Couple Therapy: Creating Connection* (NY: Routledge, 2004).

J. Kort, *Is My Husband Gay, Straight or Bi?: A Guide for Women Concerned About Their Men* (Latham, MD: Rowman & Littlefield, 2014).

P. Mellody, *Facing Love Addiction: Giving Yourself the Power to Change the Way You Love* (NY: Harper One Publishers, 2003).

P. Mellody, *The Intimacy Factor: The Ground Rules for Overcoming the Obstacles to Truth, Respect, and Lasting Love* (NY: Harper One Publishers, 2004).

S.A. Mitchell, *Can Love Last? The Fate of Romance Over Time* (NY: W. W. Norton, 2002)

R. Schwartz and J. Olds, *Marriage in Motion: The Ebb and Flow of Marriage Over Time* (Cambridge, MA: Perseus Book Group, 2000).

S. Tatkin, *We Do: Saying Yes to a Relationship of Depth, True Commitment and Enduring Love* (Louisville, CO: Sounds True, 2018).

S. Tatkin, *Wired for Love: How Understanding Your Partner's Brain and Attachment Style Can Help You Defuse Conflict and Build a Secure Relationship* (Oakland, CA: New Harbinger Publications, 2013).

R. Weiss, *Prodependence: Moving Beyond Codependency* (Deerfield Beach, FL: Health Communications, Inc., 2018).

SEXUALITY

L. Barbach, *For Yourself: The Fulfillment of Female Sexuality* (NY: New American Library, 2000).

R. Basson, "Human Sexual Response Cycles," *Journal of Sex and Marital Therapy*, 27(1), 33-43.

B. Bercaw and G. Bercaw, *The Couples Guide to Intimacy: How Sexual Reintegration Therapy Can Help Your Relationship Heal* (Pasadena, CA: CreateSpace, 2010).

L. Brotto and M. Yule, *Better Sex Through Mindfulness* (Vancouver, B.C.: Greystone Books, 2018).

K.M. Hertlein, G. R. Weeks, and S. K. Sendak, *A Clinician's Guide to Systemic Sex Therapy* (NY: Routledge, 2009).

S. Iasenza, *Transforming Sexual Narratives* (NY: Routledge, 2020).

A. Katehakis, *Erotic Intelligence* (Deerfield Beach, FL: Health Communications Inc., 1997).

A. Katehakis, *Sexual Reflections: A Workbook for Designing and Celebrating Your Sexual Health Plan* (Los Angeles, CA: Center for Healthy Sex, 2018).

A. Katehakis and Tom Bliss, *Mirror of Intimacy: Daily Reflections on Emotional and Erotic Intelligence* (Los Angeles, CA: Center for Healthy Sex, 2014).

P. J. Kleinplatz and A. Menard. *Magnificent Sex: Lessons From Extraordinary Lovers* (NY: Routledge, 2020).

B. McCarthy and E. McCarthy, *Contemporary Male Sexuality: Confronting Myths & Promoting Change* (NY: Routledge, 2020).

B. McCarthy and E. McCarthy, *Finding Your Sexual Voice: Celebrating Female Sexuality* (NY: Routledge, 2018).

B. McCarthy and E. McCarthy, *Rekindling Desire* (NY: Routledge; 3rd edition, 2019).

J. Morin, *The Erotic Mind* (NY: Harper Perennial, 1995).

E. Nagoski, *Come As You Are: The Surprising New Science* (NY: Simon & Schuster, 2015).

T. Nelson, *The New Monogamy: Redefining Your Relationship After Infidelity* (NY: New Harbinger Press, 2012).

T. Nelson, *Getting the Sex You Want: Shed Your Inhibitions and Reach New Heights of Passion Together* (Quiver, 2012).

E. Perel, *Mating in Captivity: Reconciling the Erotic & the Domestic* (NY: Harper Collins, 2006).

E. Perel, *The State of Affairs: Rethinking Infidelity* (NY: Harper Collins, 2019).

L. Weiner and C. Avery-Clark, *Sensate Focus in Sex Therapy* (NY: Routledge, 2017).

B. Zilbergeld, *The New Male Sexuality* (NY: Random House, 1999)

PSYCHOTHERAPY/ PSYCHOLOGY/ SPIRITUALITY

J. Bowlby, *A Secure Base: Parent-Child Attachment and Healthy Human Development* (NY: Basic Books, 1988).

M. Csikszentmihalyi, *Flow: The Psychology of Optimal Experience* (NY: Harper Perennial Modern Classics, 2008).

E. Fromm, *The Art of Loving* (NY: Bantam Books, 1963).

J. L. Herman, *Trauma and Recovery* (NY: Basic Books, 1992).

A. Levine and R. Heller, *Attached: The New Science of Adult Attachment & How It Can Help You Find and Keep Love* (NY: Penguin, 2010).

R. Schwartz, *Internal Family Systems Therapy* (NY: Guilford Press, 1995).

D. Siegel, M.D. *The Developing Mind* (NY: Guilford Press, 1999).

J. Kabat-Zinn, *Wherever You Go, There You Are: Mindfulness Meditation in Everyday Life* (NY: Hyperion, 1994).

RESOURCES

RECOVERY FELLOWSHIPS FOR THE HURT PARTNER AND OTHER LOVED ONES

COSA
(self-help for those affected by compulsive sexual behavior)
866-899-2672
www.cosa-recovery.org

Recovering Couples Anonymous
877-663-2317
www.recovering-couples.org

S-Anon
(self-help for those affected by another's sexual behavior)
800-210-8141
615-833-3152
www.sanon.org

Al-Anon
800-344-2666
www.al-anon.org

RECOVERY FELLOWSHIPS

Sex Addicts Anonymous (SAA)
800-477-8191
713-869-4902
www.saa-recovery.org

Sex and Love Addicts Anonymous (SLAA)
210-828-7900
www.slaafws.org

Sexaholics Anonymous (SA)
866-424-8777
www.sa.org

Sexual Recovery Anonymous (SRA)
www.sexualrecovery.org/

Sexual Compulsives Anonymous (SCA)
800-977-HEAL
www.sca-recovery.org

Porn Anonymous (PA)
www.pornanonymous.org

Pornography Addicts Anonymous (PAA)
www.pornaddictsanonymous.org/

Sex and Porn Addicts Anonymous (SPAA)
424-209-7739
www.spaa-recovery.org/

TREATMENT CENTERS AND ONLINE RESOURCES

International Institute for Trauma and Addiction Professionals (IITAP)
Carefree, AZ 85377
866-575-6853
www.sexhelp.com

American Association for Sexuality Educators, Counselors and Therapists (AASECT)
35 E. Wacker Drive, Suite 850
Chicago, IL 60601
202 449 1099
www.aasect.org

Center for Healthy Sex
10700 Santa Monica Boulevard
Los Angeles, CA 90025
310-843-9902
www.centerforhealthysex.com

The Meadows
1655 N. Tegner Street
Wickenburg, AZ 85390
800-632-3697
www.themeadows.com

Bethesda Workshops
3710 Franklin Pike
Nashville, TN 37204
615-467-5610
www.bethesdaworkshops.org

Seeking Integrity
Los Angeles, CA
747-234-HEAL (4325)
www.seekingintegrity.com

Society for the Advancement of Sexual Health (SASH)
www.sash.net
610-348-4783

Partners of Sex Addicts Blog:
Survival Strategies for Partners of Sex Addicts
www.vickitidwellpalmer.com

RESOURCES FOR LGBT FOLKS

Breathe Life Healing Centers
www.breathelifehealingcenters.com

CenterLink
www.lgbtcenters.org

The Trevor Project
www.thetrevorproject.org

ACKNOWLEDGMENTS

It takes a village to make a good therapist. I am so grateful to the village that supported my growth over the last 30 years. Attending Bruce Carruth's workshop in Rutgers more than 20 years ago introduced me to a model of what a great therapist looks like. Dr. Leon Tec—I miss your jokes and wisdom. Thanks to Sylvia Rosenfeld, Suzanne Iasenza, Esther Perel, William Granzig, and Krista Bloom, from whom I learned how to work with sexuality issues. I learned so much from the workshops and teachings of Harville Hendrix and Helen LaKelly Hunt, Sue Johnson, Tammy Nelson, John Gottman, Patrick Carnes, Rob Weiss, Alex Katehakis, Stefanie Carnes, and Stan Tatkin.

I am grateful to my colleagues who were always there with advice and support—Dana, Denise, Thea, Karen, Melissa, Janet, Theresa, and Talia. I could not have done this without the amazing editing skills of Douglas Moser and Joan Tapper, who made this a far better book, and the design talent of John Balkwill. Thanks also to the rest of my book team—James, Jennifer, Maya, and Sarah, who helped with all the skills and decisions I never knew about. I am honored by the opportunity to walk the healing journey with the individuals and couples who trusted me with their lives.

And I want to thank my patient and eternally supportive family—Marc, Alex, Sam, and Jasper.

ABOUT THE AUTHOR

Merry Frons, PhD, LCSW, CST-S, CSAT-S, CAC, is the clinical director of Renew Counseling in New York City, a practice she founded more than 25 years ago. Dr. Frons specializes in treating individuals and couples with relationship and sexuality issues and provides supervision and training for therapists. She did postdoctoral work in family and couples therapy at NYU's postdoctoral program in psychotherapy and psychoanalysis, and has extensive experience in EMDR, Imago, Gottman, and PACT relationship therapy. She enjoys working with couples because she believes that rapid and profound change is often possible. Dr. Frons and her husband have two adult children and live in Wainscott, New York.

For more information on Dr. Frons
or *The Trust Solution* resources, please see
www.thetrustsolution.com
or
www.renewcounselingpllc.com

CPSIA information can be obtained
at www.ICGtesting.com
Printed in the USA
BVHW070808131021
618829BV00001B/17